# 100 Ideas for Secondary Teachers:

# Supporting Students with ADHD

Jannine Perryman

BLOOMSBURY EDUCATION
LONDON  OXFORD  NEW YORK  NEW DELHI  SYDNEY

BLOOMSBURY EDUCATION
Bloomsbury Publishing Plc
50 Bedford Square, London, WC1B 3DP, UK
29 Earlsfort Terrace, Dublin 2, Ireland

BLOOMSBURY, BLOOMSBURY EDUCATION and the Diana logo are trademarks of Bloomsbury Publishing Plc

First published in Great Britain 2024 by Bloomsbury Publishing Ltd

This edition published in Great Britain 2024 by Bloomsbury Publishing Ltd
Text copyright © Jannine Perryman, 2024

Jannine Perryman has asserted her right under the Copyright, Designs and Patents Act, 1988, to be identified as Author of this work

Bloomsbury Publishing Plc does not have any control over, or responsibility for, any third-party websites referred to or in this book. All internet addresses given in this book were correct at the time of going to press. The author and publisher regret any inconvenience caused if addresses have changed or sites have ceased to exist, but can accept no responsibility for any such changes

All rights reserved. No part of this publication may be reproduced or transmitted in any form or by any means, electronic or mechanical, including photocopying, recording, or any information storage or retrieval system, without prior permission in writing from the publishers

A catalogue record for this book is available from the British Library

ISBN: PB: 978-1-8019-9346-3; ePDF: 978-1-8019-9344-9; ePub: 978-1-8019-9343-2

2 4 6 8 10 9 7 5 3 1 (paperback)

Typeset by Newgen KnowledgeWorks Pvt. Ltd., Chennai, India
Printed and bound in the UK by CPI Group (UK) Ltd., Croydon, CR0 4YY

To find out more about our authors and books visit www.bloomsbury.com and sign up for our newsletters

# Contents

Acknowledgements vii
Foreword by Dr Tony Lloyd viii
Introduction x
How to use this book xii

## Part 1: Understanding ADHD and wider neurodiversity 1
1. Inquisitive natures 2
2. Mental health in a neurotypical world 3
3. Trauma and adverse childhood experiences (ACEs) 4
4. The heightened risk of school-induced ACEs 5
5. Developmental delay in ADHD and autism 6
6. Co-occurrence of ADHD and autism 7
7. ADHD and dyslexia in tandem 8
8. The expanding landscape of neurodiversity 9
9. ADHD and sensory difficulties 10

## Part 2: Motivating and supporting ADHD students 13
10. Supporting learners to get started 14
11. The power of impulse 15
12. Visualising the end product 16
13. Breaking down the steps 17
14. Independent work 18
15. Future planning and focus 19
16. Problem-solving skills 20
17. Strengths and limitations of perfectionism 21
18. Perfection paralysis 22
19. Time blindness 23
20. Effective and realistic time management 24
21. Prioritisation 25
22. Overwhelm 26
23. The middle matters 27
24. Motivation 28

## Part 3: Supporting emotional and physical needs — **29**
- 25. Low-energy moments — 30
- 26. Hand fidgets — 31
- 27. Body fidgeting — 32
- 28. Toilet breaks — 33
- 29. Negative self-belief — 34
- 30. Negative self-talk — 35
- 31. Emotional dysregulation — 36
- 32. Emotional overwhelm — 37
- 33. Friendships — 38

## Part 4: Classroom management — **39**
- 34. Off-task shouting and tangents — 40
- 35. Not shouting out — 41
- 36. Classroom distractions — 42
- 37. Back to work after a distraction — 43
- 38. Inclusive seating plans — 44
- 39. Classroom chatter — 45
- 40. Low-level disruptive talking — 46
- 41. Unintended distractions — 47
- 42. Deliberate distractions — 48
- 43. Attention-seeking behaviours — 49
- 44. Low-dopamine attention-seeking — 50
- 45. Pushing boundaries — 51

## Part 5: Distractions, disruptions and disrespect — **53**
- 46. Disrespectful conduct — 54
- 47. Rule adherence — 55
- 48. Low-level persistent disruption — 56
- 49. 'Answering back' behaviour — 57
- 50. Oppositional behaviour — 58
- 51. Self-opposition — 59
- 52. Anxiety — 60

## Part 6: Memory — **61**
- 53. Working memory challenges: a mental arithmetic example — 62
- 54. Working memory challenges: multitasking for written tasks — 63
- 55. Short-term memory — 64
- 56. Long-term memory — 65
- 57. The challenge of recall — 66

## Part 7: Learning and exams — 67
- 58 Independent work planning — 68
- 59 Staying on track with assignments — 69
- 60 Revisiting work — 70
- 61 Editing — 71
- 62 Exam questions — 72
- 63 Overlooking exam questions — 73
- 64 Understanding intricate questions — 74
- 65 Handwriting challenges — 75
- 66 High-stakes handwriting — 76
- 67 Spelling, punctuation and grammar — 77
- 68 Streamlined content presentation — 78
- 69 Expanding content — 79
- 70 Word-based maths — 80
- 71 Mental arithmetic — 81
- 72 Instinctive answers — 82
- 73 Transcribing information accurately — 83
- 74 Repeated reading distractions — 84
- 75 Inattentive scan reading — 85
- 76 Misreading tendencies — 86
- 77 Speed of thought vs. hand — 87
- 78 Tech to aid writing nuances — 88

## Part 8: Impulsivity, attribution and justice — 89
- 79 Promoting impulse control — 90
- 80 Effective recovery after an impulsive act — 91
- 81 Difficulty learning from mistakes — 92
- 82 Lying to avoid conflict — 93
- 83 Owning up to mistakes — 94
- 84 Embracing restorative justice — 95
- 85 A heightened sense of justice — 96
- 86 Advocacy and over-involvement — 97
- 87 Uber empathy — 98

## Part 9: Homework, attendance and independent development — 99
- 88 Asking for and accepting help — 100
- 89 Forgetfulness — 101
- 90 Effective homework planner use — 102
- 91 Forgotten homework — 103
- 92 Homework challenges — 104
- 93 Handing in homework on time — 105
- 94 School attendance difficulties — 106

**Part 10: Working with parents and professionals** — **107**
- 95 School exclusions — 108
- 96 Zero tolerance behaviour policies — 109
- 97 Reasonable adjustments — 110
- 98 Balanced and constructive school reports — 111
- 99 Constructive parents' evenings — 112
- 100 ADHD assessment reporting scales for teachers — 113

Glossary — 114

## Dedication

To all of the young people I have taught and who have taught me in return. When writing this, many of you came to mind, I won't name names, but you know who you are.

To all of the teachers, and teaching assistants, who have had mixed blessings with working alongside me. Thank you for accepting and celebrating my differences, and my experimental approaches that have manifested in the knowledge contained in this book.

To all of the senior and middle leaders who have supported me on my journey, thank you for trusting and steering me. Even when we haven't agreed, I have learned many lessons from you.

# Acknowledgements

I would like to acknowledge the team at The ADHD Foundation, The Neurodiversity Charity, but both Dr Tony Lloyd and Colin Foley in particular. Colin was the first professional I heard speak who spoke the same language as me, and Tony for his ongoing mentorship and wisdom.

To Michele Gutteridge, for always believing in me, even when I didn't believe in myself, and Barry James for the same.

Thank you to the community that supports me online, who provided me with quotes and asked me inspiring questions. I hope I have represented you well in what I have put together.

To the teacher training team at Bedford College and University of Bedfordshire, for both stretching and supporting me, you made it both easy and difficult in the right ways, particularly Samantha Jones, my mentor, who went above and beyond and is a bastion of genuine inclusion that continues to inform my practice today.

To the team that have been part of this process, present and past: Hayley, Ruth, Claire, Becca, Charlotte and Vicky.

Thank you to Emily and Bloomsbury, for your patience and wisdom.

Last, but not least, to my children Vicki, Will and Becca, for making me who I am, and waking me up to the world of neurodiversity.

# Foreword

This book is a welcome contribution to the debate about inclusive education. What does a neurodiversity paradigm mean for pedagogy in our schools? And for a teaching profession that is adapting to the very different needs of children who are transitioning into adulthood in a rapidly changing, technology-driven world and workplace? As a former teacher, professional coach, entrepreneur, parent, and with the lived experience of a woman with ADHD and autism, Jannine Perryman brings a wealth of experience that brings the book alive.

A neuro-inclusive education system that 'enables' rather than 'disables' those young people who reflect this *diversity of mind* is the new normal. Every classroom is neurodiverse, requiring a *diversity of mindset from teachers*. This recognition will challenge many obsolete paradigms, such as our concept of intelligence, the purpose of education, and a medical model that has labelled those who think differently as disordered. ADHD and autism, like dyslexia, dyscalculia and dyspraxia, cannot be cured — nor are they meant to be.

One in ten human beings are dyslexic, one in ten have dyspraxia, one in 20 are impacted by ADHD, one in ten have dyscalculia and one in 60 are autistic. That one in five children and adults have these different minds is evidence that there is an evolutionary purpose as to why some people think differently. Neurodiversity is the universal design.

Industry is leading the way in recognising, valuing and harnessing the extraordinary talent, creative thinking, entrepreneurialism and innovation of the one in five who 'think differently'. Research suggests that over 30 per cent of business owners and entrepreneurs have either dyslexia or ADHD or both; university graduates with ADHD are twice as likely to start their own business; over 40 per cent of millionaires have dyslexia. The major growth industries of the 21st century in a rapidly changing, technology-driven economy and culture are a testament to the fact that they have been actively recruiting a neurodiverse workforce for the past three decades. This contrasts with research that states seven out of ten children excluded from our schools are those with the same different minds that industry values.[1]

---

[1] www.adhdfoundation.org.uk/wp-content/uploads/2023/06/Introducing_the_ADHD_Foundation_Neurodiversity_Charity_13.06.pdf

This book will provide a new perspective and offer practical strategies and guidance for teachers that can only benefit everyone – the profession, families and school communities – as we chart our way through the decade ahead, where the pace of change will be exponential. We need a new canon for education; the neurodiversity canon is here.

*Dr Tony Lloyd, CEO of the ADHD Foundation Neurodiversity Charity*

# Introduction

This book is an invaluable resource for secondary teachers, providing a comprehensive understanding of attention deficit hyperactivity disorder (ADHD) and its impact on young learners. It addresses the common challenge teachers face: balancing the enforcement of school rules with providing the right support to students with ADHD. The book emphasises that with appropriate support and understanding, students with ADHD can not only succeed but also excel in their educational journey.

ADHD, as a neurodevelopmental condition, affects various aspects of a student's life, including their ability to focus, control impulses, understand their emotions and manage time effectively. This book guides teachers through the nuances of these challenges, offering practical strategies to support these students' unique functioning. By understanding the underlying mechanisms of ADHD, teachers can apply methods that go beyond traditional disciplinary approaches, creating an environment where students with ADHD are encouraged and empowered.

This resource highlights the importance of a supportive classroom environment that caters to the diverse needs of all students. It suggests adaptive strategies that can enhance motivation, improve organisational skills, and foster better engagement for students with ADHD. These strategies are not only beneficial for students with ADHD but can also enrich the learning experience for the entire class.

By implementing the insights and techniques provided in this book, teachers can help students with ADHD overcome their challenges and harness their potential. It advocates for a shift in perspective, seeing ADHD not as a barrier but as a different way of learning and interacting with the world. With the right support, as this book illustrates, students with ADHD can achieve remarkable success and contribute positively to the classroom and beyond. This guide is a testament to the idea that when students with ADHD are understood and supported appropriately, they can thrive academically and personally.

**Neurotypes: An expanding understanding**

Neurodiversity is a concept that values diversity in human brains and abilities, recognising that neurological differences like ADHD are a natural variation of the human genome. The world of neurodiversity is vast and continually evolving. As our comprehension of the brain and its functions deepens, we recognise and categorise an ever-increasing range of neurotypes. The current list of diagnosable neurodiverse conditions, while extensive, continues to grow and includes:

- attention deficit hyperactivity disorder (ADHD)
- autism spectrum disorder (ASD)
- dyslexia
- dyspraxia/developmental coordination disorder (DCD)
- dysgraphia
- dyscalculia
- Tourette's syndrome (TS)
- obsessive compulsive disorder (OCD)
- sensory processing disorder (SPD)
- social communication disorder
- non-verbal learning disorder (NVLD).

The following can be considered aspects of neurodiversity and they are gaining more recognition:

- synesthesia
- bipolar disorder
- anxiety disorders
- depression
- post-traumatic stress disorder (PTSD)
- generalised anxiety disorder (GAD)
- schizophrenia.

It's paramount for educators and caregivers to stay updated on these classifications and understandings. As our knowledge expands, some conditions may be redefined, reclassified or comprehended in fresh and enlightening ways. Adopting a proactive and informed approach ensures that we provide the best possible environment and understanding for all our students.

# How to use this book

This book includes quick, easy and practical ideas for you to dip in and out of to help you support the students with ADHD in your classroom.

Each idea includes:

- A catchy title, easy to refer to and share with your colleagues.
- A quote from a teacher or a student describing their experience that has led to the idea.
- A summary of the idea in bold, making it easy to flick through the book and identify an idea you want to use at a glance.
- Multiple strategies to use with your students based around the idea.

Each idea also includes one or more of the following:

| Teaching tip | Taking it further | Bonus idea ★ |
| --- | --- | --- |
| Practical tips and advice for how and how not to run the activity or put the idea into practice. | Ideas and advice for how to extend the idea or develop it further. | There are 10 bonus ideas in this book that are extra-exciting, extra-original and extra-interesting. |

Some of the ideas have additional downloadable content, and this will be flagged using this icon in the text. You can download the content here: **bloomsbury.pub/100-ideas-secondary-ADHD**

There is a glossary at the end of the book containing some of the key terms used throughout the ideas. Terms included in the glossary are emphasised in **bold underline** throughout the book.

Share how you use these ideas and find out what other practitioners have done using **#100ideas**.

# Understanding ADHD and wider neurodiversity

Part 1

# IDEA 1

# Inquisitive natures

ADHD students don't ask 'why' just to be difficult; they need to understand the purpose to fuel their motivation and navigate their dopamine-driven brains. *Mr. Davis, Psychology Teacher*

**ADHD students often exhibit a persistent need to understand the 'why' behind tasks and instructions. This inquisitiveness is rooted in their neurochemistry, where understanding the purpose can make the difference between engagement and apathy.**

### Teaching tip

ADHD students' constant quest for 'why' is more than mere curiosity; it's a vital tool for their engagement and motivation. By providing clear rationales and fostering a classroom environment that values understanding, we can tap into this inquisitiveness, turning it into a powerful driver for learning and growth.

Here are some strategies you can try:

**Acknowledge the dopamine dilemma** Recognise that lower dopamine levels in ADHD students make it challenging to engage in tasks that seem dull or pointless without a compelling reason.

**Provide clear rationales** Whenever possible, offer clear explanations for tasks, highlighting their purpose and relevance. This helps ADHD students 'sell' the task to themselves and boosts their motivation.

**Empathise with their quest for understanding** Instead of viewing persistent questioning as defiance or distraction, see it as a genuine need for clarity and purpose.

**Encourage curiosity** While it's essential to provide clear rationales, also encourage ADHD students to remain curious, fostering a love for learning and understanding.

**Collaborative task setting** Involve ADHD students in the process of setting tasks or objectives, allowing them to see the bigger picture and understand the underlying reasons.

**IDEA 2**

# Mental health in a neurotypical world

*It's not just about focusing in class. It's the constant feeling of being out of step, different from my peers, that weighs on my mind.*
*Tasha, 16*

**ADHD students face a myriad of mental health challenges, amplified by the daily reminder of being different in a world designed for <u>neurotypical</u> minds. The intersection of their inherent neurological differences and external societal pressures creates a unique set of emotional and psychological hurdles.**

Here are some strategies you can try:

**Acknowledge the difference** Understand that for ADHD students, feelings of being different can be a significant source of stress, affecting their self-perception and mental health.

**Spotting signs** Be vigilant in recognising signs of distress stemming from social isolation, peer comparison or perceived inadequacy, including spending break times alone or a change in eating habits.

**Foster acceptance** Create an inclusive classroom environment that celebrates neurodiversity, helping ADHD students embrace their unique strengths and challenges. See the Bloomsbury Education website for a lesson plan explaining this.

**Peer education** Educate the entire class about ADHD, fostering understanding and reducing potential stigmatisation or misconceptions.

**Empower and affirm** Regularly affirm ADHD students, emphasising their value and unique contributions, ensuring they feel seen and appreciated in their entirety.

### Teaching tip

Embracing neurodiversity in the classroom isn't just about understanding ADHD; it's about recognising the emotional toll of feeling 'different' and actively working to bridge that gap. By creating an environment of acceptance and understanding, and by thinking about how you can include neurodiversity in your subject, you can help ADHD students navigate their challenges with confidence and resilience.

# IDEA 3

# Trauma and adverse childhood experiences (ACEs)

The interplay between ADHD and trauma can be profound, with **ACEs** amplifying challenges for our students. Recognising and addressing this intersection is crucial for creating a supportive and healing educational environment. *Mr. Walton, Special Educational Needs Coordinator (SENCO)*

For ADHD students, trauma, often stemming from ACEs, can compound the challenges they face. The overlap between ADHD symptoms and trauma responses necessitates a comprehensive and compassionate approach to support.

Here are some strategies you can try:

**Understanding ACEs** Familiarise yourself with the common ACEs, from physical and emotional abuse to school-related adversity like exclusions or attendance difficulties.

**Recognise the overlap** Understand that many symptoms of ADHD, such as impulsivity or emotional dysregulation, can also be trauma responses. Differentiating between the two is crucial for effective intervention.

**Safe spaces** Create an environment where ADHD students can express their feelings and experiences without judgement, ensuring they feel heard, validated and supported.

**Trauma-informed practices** Incorporate strategies that are sensitive to trauma, such as predictable routines, clear boundaries and regular check-ins.

**Collaborative support** Engage with parents, caregivers and professionals to ensure a holistic approach to the student's wellbeing, addressing both ADHD and trauma-related needs.

> **Teaching tip**
>
> Addressing the dual challenges of ADHD and trauma requires a deep well of empathy, understanding and flexibility. By recognising the profound impact of ACEs and tailoring our support to address both ADHD and trauma, we can provide our students with the tools they need to heal and thrive.

**IDEA 4**

# The heightened risk of school-induced ACEs

It's a difficult truth to face, recognising that our system can sometimes fail our ADHD students, exposing them to unintended traumas. Addressing this head-on is the only way we can affect meaningful change. *Mr. Davies, SENCO*

**ACEs within schools can inadvertently affect any student. However, those with ADHD, due to their unique neurological and behavioural profiles, are often at a heightened risk of experiencing these traumas.**

Here are some strategies you can try:

**Recognise the vulnerability** Understand that ADHD students, due to their impulsivity, hyperactivity and inattentiveness, can often be misunderstood, leading to punitive measures or unintentional neglect.

**Awareness of past traumas** Realise that ADHD students might have previous school-induced ACEs, making them more reactive or seeking to test the waters for further rejections.

**Open dialogue** Ensure that students with ADHD have platforms to express their feelings, experiences and concerns without fear, fostering a sense of validation.

**Responsive actions** Address incidents with empathy and understanding, ensuring that ADHD students feel their unique challenges are recognised and respected.

**Build trust** Understand that rebuilding trust with ADHD students who've experienced trauma might require tailored approaches, patience and consistent effort.

> **Teaching tip**
>
> The unique challenges faced by ADHD students mean they are often more susceptible to negative school experiences. By being informed, understanding and proactive, we can reduce the risk of school-induced ACEs for these students, ensuring a supportive and inclusive educational environment for all.

# IDEA 5

# Developmental delay in ADHD and autism

People expect me to act my age, but sometimes it's hard. I wish they understood that my brain works a bit differently. *Sam, 13*

**Students with ADHD and autism often experience a 20–30 per cent developmental delay in areas of <u>executive function</u> and emotional maturity. Recognising this delay and adjusting our expectations is crucial to providing appropriate support, ensuring we bridge any gaps in their learning journey.**

Here are some strategies you can try:

**Recognise the delay** Understand that the typical developmental delay in ADHD and autism can make age-appropriate responses challenging for some students.

**Adjust expectations** While maintaining high standards, adjust your expectations based on the student's developmental stage, not just their chronological age.

**Identify strengths and weaknesses** Recognise that these students often have a 'spiky' profile, excelling in some areas while struggling in others.

**Tailor support** Provide targeted support in areas of delay, while also leveraging their strengths to foster self-confidence.

**Bridge learning gaps** Identify and address academic and other learning gaps that arise due to developmental delays.

**Promote self-awareness** Help students understand their developmental profile, fostering self-awareness and self-advocacy.

**Collaborate with specialists** Engage with SEN specialists to gain insights and strategies for supporting students effectively.

### Taking it further

It's important to adopt a strength-based perspective when addressing developmental delay in ADHD. By highlighting and nurturing students' innate capabilities, we can not only boost their self-confidence but also provide them with tools to navigate and manage the challenges of their developmental lag. Emphasising strengths doesn't mean ignoring the delays; instead, it offers a balanced view that recognises the complete range of a student's abilities.

# IDEA 6

# Co-occurrence of ADHD and autism

When working with students diagnosed with ADHD or autism, it's crucial to remain open to the possibility of co-occurrence. Recognising the interplay between these conditions can help us provide more tailored and effective support. *Mr. Thompson, SENCO*

**The co-occurrence of ADHD and autism, though varied in reported rates among studies, offers a unique set of challenges and strengths for affected students. Recognising the potential overlap and understanding the nuanced interplay between these conditions is vital for educators aiming to provide comprehensive support.**

Here are some strategies you can try:

**Stay informed** Familiarise yourself with the latest research on the co-occurrence of ADHD and autism to better understand the complexities.

**Be observant** Look out for signs that suggest a student may have traits of both conditions, even if they are only diagnosed with one.

**Acknowledge individuality** Each student will present their unique combination of ADHD and autism traits; tailor your support accordingly.

**Encourage open dialogue** Foster an environment where students feel comfortable discussing their feelings, experiences and challenges related to their diagnoses.

**Stay flexible** Co-occurrence can lead to atypical presentations. Adapt your strategies based on the evolving needs of the student.

**Holistic approach** Recognise that while you may not always be able to attribute specific traits to one condition or the other, every trait contributes to the student's overall identity.

**Seek specialist support** Collaborate with SENCOs, educational psychologists and therapists familiar with both conditions to provide the best support.

### Teaching tip

Remember that your role is not to label or compartmentalise, but to understand and support. Embracing the complexities of co-occurring ADHD and autism can enable you to connect more deeply with your students and facilitate their academic and personal growth.

## IDEA 7

# ADHD and dyslexia in tandem

*My ADHD makes me think outside the box, and my dyslexia means I see the world differently. Together, they make me who I am, even if school can be tough sometimes.* Malik, 12

**The co-occurrence of ADHD and dyslexia presents a unique blend of cognitive strengths and challenges. For educators, understanding the synergies and conflicts between these conditions is essential for providing effective and empathetic support.**

### Teaching tip

Seeing beyond the challenges to recognise the unique strengths of students with ADHD and dyslexia can transform their educational experience. Our role is to champion their potential, provide tailored support, and celebrate their achievements, no matter how big or small.

### Taking it further

Tracking can be difficult with ADHD and dyslexia co-occurrence, especially when transferring information from one medium to another. Recognise this challenge and proactively adapt your teaching methods. Use technology such as text-to-speech tools or dictation software, provide printouts of lessons, or offer audio recordings. These alternatives ensure that students genuinely access, engage with and comprehend the learning material and assessments.

Here are some strategies you can try:

**Stay updated about ADHD about dyslexia** The ADHD Foundation and BDA website are trusted places to seek advice and there is further information on the Bloomsbury Education website.

**Recognise overlaps** Be aware that certain behaviours or challenges might be attributed to both conditions, such as inattention or difficulties with reading – especially tracking.

**Celebrate strengths** Emphasise the creative thinking, problem-solving abilities and unique perspectives often present in students with both ADHD and dyslexia.

**Tailor instruction** Differentiate teaching methods to cater to individual needs, like using visual aids, interactive activities or technology.

**Promote self-understanding** Help students understand their dual diagnosis, fostering self-awareness and self-advocacy skills.

**Provide multi-sensory learning** Incorporate various sensory inputs in lessons to cater to different learning styles and needs.

**Seek collaborative support** Work with SENCOs, educational psychologists and dyslexia specialists to develop targeted strategies and interventions.

**Foster peer understanding** Educate classmates about ADHD and dyslexia, promoting an inclusive and supportive classroom environment.

# IDEA 8

# The expanding landscape of neurodiversity

Embracing neurodiversity is not just about accepting differences, but about celebrating the myriad ways in which our brains function and interpret the world. *Mr. Thompson, Head of Inclusion*

**Neurodiversity, a term that encapsulates the diverse range of human neurocognitive functioning, is gradually shifting perceptions from deficit-focused views to a more inclusive understanding of difference. With ADHD being a part of this rich spectrum, it's essential to recognise its value and the broader context of neurodiversity in our evolving understanding.**

Here are some strategies you can try:

**Shift the paradigm** Move from a deficit model to one that recognises and celebrates diverse neurological functioning as natural variations of the human experience.

**Broaden perspectives** Approximately 30 per cent of the population can be considered neurodivergent, underscoring the prevalence and importance of diverse neurological experiences.

**Promote inclusion** Create an inclusive environment where students of all neurotypes feel valued and understood.

**Educate the community** Raise awareness about neurodiversity, ensuring that staff, students and the broader community understand the concept and its implications.

**Celebrate strengths** Identify and uplift the unique strengths and abilities that come with different neurotypes, including ADHD.

**Seek collaboration** Engage with specialists, advocacy groups and neurodivergent individuals to gain insights and develop supportive strategies.

**Be flexible** What works for one neurodivergent individual might not work for another.

### Teaching tip

Remember, the term neurodiversity encompasses us all, not just those with diagnosed conditions. By recognising and valuing the full range of neurological experiences, we can foster a more understanding, compassionate and enriched educational environment.

A list of what is currently considered to be neurodiversity can be found in the introduction.

# IDEA 9

# ADHD and sensory difficulties

The classroom can sometimes feel overwhelming, not just because of the work, but because of all the sounds, sensations and things happening around me. It's like my senses are always turned up to maximum. *Liam, 14*

**Students with ADHD often grapple with an array of sensory difficulties that can significantly influence their learning experience. From <u>proprioception</u> to <u>auditory processing disorder</u>, these issues require understanding, adjustments and supportive interventions.**

> **Teaching tip**
>
> While it may seem that a student is 'coping' in a sensory-rich environment, it's crucial to recognise the immense effort and energy they might be expending to do so. By being proactive and making necessary adjustments, you can reduce the sensory overload and help students focus on their learning, rather than just 'coping'.

Here are some strategies you can try:

**Recognise the spectrum** Understand that sensory difficulties can range from sensory-seeking behaviours to sensory avoidant tendencies.

**Acknowledge proprioceptive challenges** Be aware that students might struggle with understanding the position and movement of their bodies, which can affect coordination and spatial awareness.

**Understand interoceptive difficulties** Recognise that some students may have trouble perceiving internal bodily sensations, making it challenging to identify feelings like hunger, thirst or the need to use the toilet.

**Don't take it personally** Realise that sensory difficulties can be overwhelming and result in unwanted behaviour. If this happens, rather than reacting to the behaviour, do your best to reduce the demands on the student so that they can regulate themselves.

**Address auditory processing** Students might find it difficult to differentiate or process auditory information, especially in noisy environments. Adjustments, such as using microphones (in assemblies), white noise in dining halls, or reducing background noise, can be beneficial, but there is a lot to be said for understanding that if you are trying to communicate in a noisy space, they just might not be able to hear you.

**Create sensory-friendly environments**
Consider the sensory demands of places like dining halls, sports areas and classrooms. Providing noise-cancelling headphones and quiet zones, or using soft lighting, can make a difference.

**Collaborate with specialists** Work with occupational therapists or sensory integration specialists to devise effective strategies and interventions.

**Educate and advocate** Inform other staff members and students about sensory difficulties associated with ADHD and wider neurodiversity, promoting understanding and fostering a supportive school community. You can learn more at www.otforkids.co.uk/conditions/sensory-processing-disorder-spd.php.

**Seek feedback** Involve students in the process of identifying triggers and creating supportive solutions, ensuring their comfort and wellbeing.

### Taking it further

Physical touch and personal space can be complex for children with sensory issues. For example, some children may benefit from a weighted blanket. Other children may find any physical touch to be distressing, perhaps being better suited to sitting a small distance away from others. It is important to communicate with the other adults they interact with regularly, such as parents or other teachers to ascertain what suits the child in different environments.

# Motivating and supporting ADHD students

Part 2

# IDEA 10

# Supporting learners to get started

It's crucial to understand that every student's starting point is different. Our task is to find where they're comfortable and guide them forward. *Mr. Smith, Maths Teacher*

**Starting a task can be an uphill battle for many students, especially those with ADHD. Recognising the narrow and fluctuating 'zone of proximal development' (ZPD) in these students is vital for their progress.**

Here are some strategies you can try:

### Identify needs

- Reflect on what the student might require to begin a task.
- Engage with the student: their insights, even if unclear, can guide the way.

### Task structuring

- Determine if the task's scope is clear.
- Break it into digestible parts – beginning, middle and end – ensuring each step is transparent.

### Ensure relevance

- Gauge if the task resonates with the student's interests.
- If it seems abstract, connect it to broader, relatable objectives.

### Adjust task difficulty

- Assess if the task's challenge level is suitable.
- Modify accordingly, ensuring it's neither too easy nor too overwhelming.

---

**Teaching tip**

Always celebrate small victories. Acknowledging a student's effort to start a task, even if not completed, can boost their confidence and motivation for future tasks.

# IDEA 11

# The power of impulse

I just want to get things done. Why wait when you can just start?
*Ben, 15*

**For students with ADHD, the impulse to jump right into a task can be both a gift and a challenge. While this eagerness can lead to rapid task initiation, it's essential they also pause and ensure they've understood the task requirements and potential obstacles.**

Here are some strategies you can try:

**Clarity is key** Before starting, ask the student, 'Can you tell me what you're planning to do?' This ensures they've grasped the task and allows for corrections if needed.

**Quick planning session** Encourage a brief moment of planning. Ask, 'Have you considered how you're going to approach this?' This promotes a mix of spontaneity and strategy.

**Harness their energy** Recognise that when they're motivated, students with ADHD can be incredibly productive. Provide positive reinforcement that celebrates their enthusiasm without imposing unrealistic expectations.

**Stay flexible** Remember, every student is unique. What works for one might not work for another. Be prepared to adapt and find what best supports each individual.

**Feedback, not pressure** Instead of saying 'You can do it when you put your mind to it', consider phrases like 'I'm really impressed with how you tackled that!' Positive reinforcement without pressure can boost their confidence.

### Teaching tip

Consider introducing short, structured planning sessions at the start of tasks. These sessions can act as a bridge between impulsivity and thoughtful action, helping students to harness the best of both worlds.

# IDEA 12

# Visualising the end product

*Sometimes it is like I can see what I want something to be like, but it's like I overthink it, and then I can't start. Beth, 14*

**Typically, learners with ADHD will either see all of the possibilities in the task before them or none. It will depend on how well the learner can relate to the stimuli, and how relevant it feels to their lives. Both of these options present a challenge and have different potential solutions. Visualising an end goal is known to be a particular challenge for some ADHD students, so be ready with examples as you plan.**

### Taking it further

According to neuropsychologist Russell Barkley, challenges with working memory can include difficulties with visualising and holding images in mind for a goal-directed purpose – yet ADHDers are usually very visual thinkers. The difficulty, then, is creating a particular visual for a goal or purpose, and holding it in mind. Aim to provide an opportunity to talk through their ideas or clarify what they would like to achieve and then put steps in place to help them get there.

If the learner can't see what an end product might look like, show them examples. ADHD students are typically very visual; showing them a few options should make it easier for them to work out how they want their work to end up.

Look to find any connection to their interests and be prepared to shift your expectations. It might be possible for them to meet the learning objective in another way.

If the learner is seeing too many possibilities, be clear on the criteria (learning objective), and ask them which of their ideas best suits what is being asked – while still captivating their interest (dopamine).

Praise the imagination and creative thought and make it clear that future opportunities to express ideas will be given.

Give students sticky notes or draft paper to work through their ideas. Depending on their idea and the task requirements, talk to them about perfect vs. done (see **Ideas 17** and **18**) and where the task sits within that.

Scaffolding such as breaking down the steps (see **Idea 13**) and a template and/or prompt sheet can be very helpful.

# IDEA 13

# Breaking down the steps

I know this is what I need to do, but my brain just wants to take me to the end, without the steps. *Magda, 14*

**Demonstrate and model how to break tasks down into steps, until students can do it for themselves.**

Imagine you have a piece of string and you are holding one end in each hand. The string represents the task, with one end being the beginning and the other being the completed task – sometimes known as forward chaining. The ADHD brain will want to go from one to the other in the quickest way possible, but there are stages they must go through and there are no shortcuts. Just as you would use clips or pegs to secure a piece of string along its journey, you need to do the same with tasks.

State each step, from the beginning to the end, clearly and simply in a way that is achievable. The number of steps will vary depending on the complexity of the task and the capacity of the child. Manageable chunks are really important to avoid overwhelm and keep the child on task. A tick list or other trackable visual can be really helpful.

Many learners benefit from visuals and checklists, so they are a good idea to have on the board for all students, maybe with some differentiation for those who need a separate hand-out version.

Distractions happen, and these strategies will help with your classroom management too. It is easier to refocus a learner if they know how to pick up where they left off.

### Taking it further

'Jet propelled thinking' is when students can go from the question to the correct answer in one seamless step, but cannot break it down. A classic example is in maths questions where they are asked to 'show your working'. Students may not know how they knew it, they just did. Considering the **executive function** required to do this, I would argue that we should only be asking it when they are making errors and need to learn something from the process. You will have to take a view on what is best for the student in light of exam requirements.

# IDEA 14

# Independent work

I either get super excited and think I can do everything, or I just can't find the motivation if it doesn't feel relevant. Finding that middle ground, where I'm optimistic but also realistic, is tricky. *Ellie, 15*

**Project and independent work present a balancing act for ADHD students. Their perception of time and approach to projects can differ from their peers. Their enthusiasm can propel them into ambitious plans, but challenges like time blindness (see Idea 19), adherence to criteria, and fluctuating idea generation can skew expectations. Celebrate their unique perspectives while offering scaffolding, to ensure their optimism is anchored in achievable goals.**

These strategies can help transform students' boundless enthusiasm into projects that meet criteria and showcase their unique insights:

**Time management workshops** Offer sessions focusing on the concept of time, helping ADHD students better gauge durations and plan accordingly.

**Clear criteria breakdown** Just as with assignments, provide detailed discussions on project criteria, ensuring students understand boundaries and expectations.

**Organise brainstorming sessions** For those overwhelmed with ideas, it can help filter and focus; for others, it can spark inspiration.

**Relevance** Engage students in discussions about the project's relevance. Helping them find personal connections can boost motivation and idea generation.

**Regular check-ins** Schedule periodic reviews of project progress. These check-ins can help students recalibrate their plans, ensuring a blend of optimism and realism.

### Taking it further

Granting time extensions for homework and coursework can be a valuable accommodation to help students process, organise and complete tasks to the best of their abilities. Extensions can alleviate undue stress, allowing students to work at a pace that aligns more closely with their cognitive processing speed, ultimately leading to improved quality of work. However, regularly extended deadlines might inadvertently reinforce procrastination, reduce urgency and foster dependency. Balancing the genuine needs of certain students with maintaining an environment of equity and skill development is crucial when considering time extensions.

# IDEA 15

# Future planning and focus

I often get told I'm 'living in the moment', which I guess is true. It's hard for me to think about next week when today feels so immediate and consuming. *Connor, 16*

**Students with ADHD often experience challenges in forward-thinking and delaying immediate rewards for future benefits. This tendency to live in the present moment, while sometimes advantageous, can impede long-term planning and the ability to work towards distant goals.**

Here are some strategies you can try:

**Visual timelines** Use visual aids like calendars, planners and timelines to help students visualise the future and map out tasks.

**Break tasks down** Divide larger, long-term tasks into smaller, more immediate steps. This makes them more manageable and provides frequent short-term rewards.

**Use rewards** Implement a system of immediate rewards for small milestones, gradually increasing the delay as students progress.

**Practise delayed gratification** Engage students in exercises specifically designed to strengthen this skill, like the classic 'marshmallow test' (see the Bonus Idea).

**Reminders and alarms** Encourage the use of digital tools and alarms to remind students of upcoming responsibilities.

**Discuss consequences** Engage in discussions about the potential future outcomes of present actions, both positive and negative.

**Role play scenarios** Use role play to help students practise future planning and understand the consequences of their choices.

**Connect present to future** Help students draw connections between their current actions and their future goals.

### Teaching tip

Recognise the strengths of living in the present, such as heightened creativity and adaptability. While guiding ADHD students towards better future planning, also celebrate these unique qualities they bring to the classroom. Offering consistent support, while also encouraging autonomy, can help them navigate the balance between the present and the future.

### Bonus idea

In the marshmallow test a child is offered one small but immediate reward or two small rewards if they wait. Choosing to wait is a measure of their ability to delay gratification and it can be a practical exercise for ADHD students to learn the value of working towards a more a long-term goal.

# IDEA 16

# Problem-solving skills

I've been astounded by the ingenious solutions some of my ADHD students come up with. Their lateral thinking often brings a fresh perspective to problems. But this ability needs nurturing, as their fear of criticism can hold them back. *Mr. Smith, Maths Teacher*

**Students with ADHD often possess an innate ability for lateral and out-of-the-box thinking, making them natural problem solvers. However, due to past experiences and fear of criticism, they might hold back from showcasing this strength.**

> **Teaching tip**
>
> Remember that for ADHD students, the process is as important as the end result, if not more so. By focusing on nurturing their problem-solving skills and building their confidence, you can help them unlock their full potential. Being transparent about your own mistakes and showing a resilient, solution-focused approach can set a positive example for them to follow.

Here are some strategies you can try:

**Encourage lateral thinking** Set tasks that don't have a single 'right' answer, allowing students to approach them in multiple ways.

**Create a safe environment** Foster a classroom atmosphere where making mistakes is seen as a learning opportunity rather than a failure.

**Reward creativity** Celebrate unique solutions and approaches, even if they don't lead to the desired outcome.

**Group work** Group activities can help ADHD students share their unique perspectives and build confidence.

**Teach reflective practices** Encourage students to reflect on what went well and what could be improved.

**Provide constructive feedback** Instead of pointing out what's wrong, guide students to find the solution themselves.

**Embrace mistakes** Highlight famous mistakes in history that led to great discoveries, emphasising the importance of perseverance.

# IDEA 17

# Strengths and limitations of perfectionism

I want everything I do to be perfect. But sometimes I get so stuck on making it just right that I end up not doing it at all. *Jamie, 14*

**Perfectionism in ADHD students can be a powerful motivator, driving them to produce outstanding work. However, it can also lead to 'perfection paralysis' (see Idea 18) where the fear of not meeting their own high standards becomes a barrier.**

Here are some strategies you can try:

**Reframe perfection** Teach students that perfection is subjective and that continuous growth is more important.

**Break tasks down** Encourage breaking tasks into smaller chunks to prevent feeling overwhelmed.

**Celebrate progress** Highlight the importance of the journey and the effort, and not just the end result.

**Foster safe spaces** Create environments where mistakes are seen as learning opportunities, not failures.

**Encourage risk taking** Allow students to step outside their comfort zones without the fear of criticism.

### Teaching tip

Remind students that everyone, including teachers, makes mistakes and that these are vital for learning and growth. Encouraging a growth mindset, where effort and progress are valued over perfection, can help alleviate the pressures of perfectionism.

# IDEA 18

# Perfection paralysis

Perfection paralysis can be both an asset and an adversary for ADHD students. Their pursuit of precision is admirable, but it's essential to guide them in understanding that striving for growth is just as valuable. *Mr. Osborne, History Teacher*

**For many ADHD students, perfection paralysis can feel like being trapped in a loop of high standards and fear of imperfections. While aiming for excellence can be a driving force, the overwhelming fear of flaws can inhibit progress and creativity.**

### Teaching tip

Integrate mindfulness techniques into the classroom. Guided imagery or visualisation exercises can help students break free from the grip of perfection paralysis by focusing on the present moment and the task at hand.

Here are some strategies you can try:

**Normalise perfection paralysis** Begin by letting students know that they are not alone in their feelings. Many people, **neurotypical** or not, struggle with perfectionism.

**Establish realistic expectations** Encourage students to set achievable goals for themselves, emphasising the idea that 'done' can sometimes be better than 'perfect'.

**Focus on process over product** Guide students to value the learning process itself, rather than just the final product.

**Mindset-shift workshops** Organise workshops or sessions that focus on shifting from a fixed mindset to a growth mindset.

**Provide constructive feedback** Ensure that feedback emphasises effort and growth. Praise dedication and resilience rather than just the end result.

**Use visual aids** Use graphs, charts or timelines to show progress over time, making the journey tangible.

**IDEA 19**

# Time blindness

Everything feels immediate or infinitely distant. I usually remember assignments only when they're imminent or ages away, but nothing in between *Mia, 15*

**Time blindness, prevalent among ADHD students, manifests as difficulties in grasping, managing and gauging time. For them, life often operates in two distinct time zones: 'now' and 'not now', making planning, prioritising and meeting deadlines challenging.**

Here are some strategies you can try:

**Visual aids** Use calendars, planners and visual schedules to make the abstract nature of time more tangible.

**Task fragmentation** Aid students in breaking projects into smaller tasks with their own deadlines, fostering urgency.

**Employ timers and alarms** Suggest the use of timers for tasks, offering a tangible sense of time passing.

**Routine and predictability** Cultivate a regular routine, helping students develop an innate sense of time.

**Real-time estimation activities** In particular subjects, devise tasks that require students to estimate time. For example, in PE, ask students to predict how long it will take them to run around the gym or change after the class. In maths or PSHE, ask them to estimate the duration of various tasks. A PSHE lesson plan example is included for this on the Bloomsbury Education website. These exercises can be enlightening and help students get a better grasp on time. They can then use this new understanding of their difficulty to be more realistic with themselves.

### Teaching tip

Schedule consistent check-ins or reminders about impending deadlines. Regular nudges can help students stay on track and diminish the stress associated with the sudden realisation of 'not now' tasks becoming 'now' tasks.

# IDEA 20

# Effective and realistic time management

*I always feel like time just slips away from me. I need strategies that make sense to my brain, not just a regular timetable. Matthew, 14*

**For ADHD students, understanding and managing time can feel like trying to grasp water. It's crucial to approach time management in a way that is both effective and tailored to their unique perception of time.**

### Teaching tip

Consider creating a classroom 'time tracker' board. Students can place tasks on the board and move them as they progress. This gives them a tangible representation of time and tasks, and also allows teachers to quickly see where a student might be struggling.

Here are some strategies you can try:

**Chunking tasks** Encourage students to break tasks down, as described in **Idea 19**.

**Visual timelines** Use visual aids like **Gantt charts** or colour-coded schedules, allowing students to see the progression of tasks over time.

**Prioritisation techniques** Teach students to categorise tasks based on urgency and importance. The **Eisenhower box** (an example is included for this on the Bloomsbury Education website) or the **ABCD method** can be helpful.

**Practice estimations** Regularly have students estimate how long they think a task will take and then compare it to the actual time. This can help them become more accurate in their predictions.

**Set clear, achievable goals** Guide students in setting **SMART** (specific, measurable, achievable, relevant, time-bound) goals, which can offer clarity and motivation.

**Regular breaks** Encourage the 'Pomodoro technique', where students use a timer to work intensively for a set period, take a short movement break, then begin again. This can help maintain focus, prevent burnout and give the student more confidence in their ability to complete things.

# IDEA 21

# Prioritisation

I know I need to do my homework, finish my project and revise for my test, but it all feels like it needs to be done NOW. How do I decide what to do first? *Sophia, 15*

**For ADHD students, the challenge of prioritisation is magnified by time blindness and the innate feeling that every task holds equal weight. Crafting strategies that respect their unique perception of time and urgency is pivotal to helping them manage their workload effectively.**

Here are some strategies you can try:

**List making** Encourage students to jot down all their tasks. This can help declutter their mind and provide a visual aid.

**Categorising tasks** Introduce the concept of the **Eisenhower box** or the **urgent–important matrix** to help them categorise tasks based on their urgency and importance.

**Visualisation techniques** Use a priority pyramid or a pie chart, where the most crucial tasks are at the top or take up the most space. This provides a visual representation of importance.

**Time estimations** Have students estimate how long each task will take. This can help them allocate adequate time to each one.

**Daily focus task** Ask students to choose one primary task that they aim to complete each day, ensuring they achieve at least one priority.

**Review and reflect** At the end of each week, spend time with students reviewing what they achieved and what felt overwhelming. This can provide insights into their prioritisation challenges.

---

**Bonus idea** ★

Create a classroom 'Priority Wall' where students can post tasks and move them around based on their changing perceptions of urgency. This not only helps the student but allows educators to offer guidance on task prioritisation. It also demonstrates that this is difficult for many, and provides an opportunity for them to learn from each other.

**IDEA 22**

# Overwhelm

In a world bursting with demands and distractions, teaching our ADHD students when to say 'no' and where to allocate their energy is as crucial as any academic lesson. *Mr. Hughes, Science Teacher*

**The modern educational landscape often leaves ADHD students feeling inundated with tasks and commitments. It's imperative to equip them with the discernment to navigate their priorities and the permission to focus on what aligns with their goals.**

Here are some strategies you can try:

**Teach prioritisation** Help students recognise which tasks and subjects align with their long-term goals and which ones, though necessary, might not require perfection.

**Empower decision-making** Encourage students to understand that it's okay to say 'no' to certain commitments or opportunities if they detract from their primary focus.

**Break down assignments** Assist students in deconstructing larger tasks into smaller steps, reducing feelings of being overwhelmed.

**Visual aids** Promote the use of planners and visual tools to map out tasks and commitments, providing clarity.

**Mindfulness and reflection** Integrate short mindfulness sessions to help students centre themselves, coupled with reflection on where their time is best spent.

**Embrace imperfection** Reinforce the message that not every subject or task needs to be approached with the same intensity. It's okay to give more to what truly matters to them.

> **Teaching tip**
>
> Hold periodic 'goal review' sessions, where students can discuss their aspirations and the subjects or tasks that are vital for reaching those aspirations. This can provide clarity and motivation for ADHD students.

**IDEA 23**

# The middle matters

The journey from the starting point to the finish line is filled with invaluable lessons. It's not just about beginning and ending; it's the middle that often teaches the most. *Ms. Barnes, Maths Teacher*

**For ADHD students, the allure of diving into a project and the satisfaction of seeing it complete are strong motivators. Yet the crucial middle steps, with their detailed processes and sustained effort, can often seem daunting or even superfluous to them.**

Here are some strategies you can try:

**Value the process** Reinforce that the middle steps are where the real learning and growth happen. It's not just a bridge from start to finish, but an essential part of the journey.

**Chunking tasks** Break tasks into manageable pieces, highlighting the importance and relevance of each step.

**Visualise the middle** Use visual aids like flow charts or storyboards to help students see and understand the sequence of steps and their importance.

**Set mini-goals** Create intermediate milestones that give a sense of accomplishment throughout the process.

**Celebrate progress** Recognise and praise efforts made during the middle phases, not just the completion of a task.

**Provide consistent feedback** Regular check-ins can keep students on track and help them see the value of their ongoing efforts.

**Connect with real-life scenarios** Use real-world examples where shortcuts can have negative implications, emphasising the importance of following through.

> **Bonus idea** ★
>
> Introduce a 'Middle Mastery' badge or award in the classroom, celebrating students who demonstrate dedication and resilience in working through the often challenging middle steps of a project or task.

## IDEA 24

# Motivation

It's not that I don't want to succeed. Sometimes, my brain just doesn't get the 'why' behind the effort. *Jamie, 16*

**For ADHD students, the landscape of motivation is intricately tied to the nuances of their dopamine reward systems. In the challenging environment of secondary schools, it's crucial to strike a balance between their intrinsic and extrinsic motivations.**

### Teaching tip

Intrinsic motivation is the internal drive to do something for its inherent satisfaction. It is a pivotal element in enhancing self-efficacy in ADHD students.

### Bonus idea ★

Create an 'Intrinsic Inspiration Board' in the classroom, where students can pin images, quotes or notes related to what personally motivates them. This visual reminder can serve as a constant source of inspiration.

Here are some strategies you can try:

**Recognise the dopamine factor** Understand that inconsistent dopamine rewards can make sustained motivation a challenge for ADHD students.

**Tap into personal interests** Boost intrinsic motivation by weaving in elements related to what individual ADHD students are passionate about.

**Offer immediate rewards** Enhance extrinsic motivation with clear, immediate rewards.

**Prioritise feedback** Regular, positive feedback can serve as a dopamine boost, reinforcing motivation.

**Maintain a balance** While immediate rewards can help in the short term, nurturing intrinsic motivation is essential for long-term growth. Try introducing a 'Topic of Choice' segment in lessons, allowing students to delve into a subject they're passionate about. This can spark intrinsic motivation and provide a platform for them to shine.

# Supporting emotional and physical needs

Part 3

# IDEA 25

# Low-energy moments

We all have days when pushing through seems impossible. For our ADHD students, these 'bare minimum' days can be frequent and are often linked to a cocktail of low interest, depleted energy and a struggle to see the bigger picture. *Ms. Lyons, School Wellbeing Coordinator*

ADHD students occasionally experience days where their drive dips significantly, resulting in output that might be perceived as minimalistic or lacking effort. These moments, often stemming from a complex interplay of low dopamine levels, emotional dysregulation and an inability to connect with the task's relevance, require understanding and tailored support.

### Teaching tip

Empathy is paramount on 'bare minimum' days. Remember, it's not about laziness or defiance. It's about an internal battle where desire to do well clashes with neurodivergent challenges. By providing an environment of understanding and flexibility, you offer ADHD students a lifeline on days when they may feel adrift.

Here are some strategies you can try:

**Acknowledge and validate** Recognise these low-energy days without judgement, offering validation and understanding to the student.

**Flexible task management** On such days, consider breaking tasks into smaller, more manageable chunks, allowing students to accomplish bits at their own pace.

**Interest-driven approaches** Whenever possible, tweak tasks to align more closely with the student's interests, providing a potential dopamine boost.

**Rest and regulate** Recognise the importance of breaks and downtime, allowing students moments to recharge and recalibrate.

**Relevance discussions** Engage in conversations about the 'why' behind tasks, helping students to see the bigger picture and potentially reigniting their motivation.

**IDEA 26**

# Hand fidgets

When I fidget, I feel more 'here'. It's like my brain switches on a bit more, and I can concentrate better. *Eli, Year 7 Student*

**Fidgeting, especially with hand tools, is a crucial coping mechanism for many ADHD students, aiding in concentration and task engagement. The subtle movements stimulate dopamine production, which in turn enhances focus and attentiveness.**

Here are some strategies you can try:

**Recognise the need** Understand that hand fidgeting is not merely a distraction but serves an essential purpose for ADHD students, aiding in increasing dopamine flow.

**Classroom-friendly fidgets** Introduce classroom-appropriate fidget tools, such as stress balls, spiral bands, fidget cubes or sticky tack. These tools can provide the necessary stimulation without causing distractions.

**Educate on responsible use** Teach students the appropriate times and ways to use their fidgets, ensuring they enhance learning rather than disrupt it.

**Affirm the importance** Refer to experts, such as Fintan O'Reagan, who liken taking away a hand fidget from an ADHD student to taking away a pen and expecting them to write. Highlight the essential nature of fidgeting for certain students.

**Monitor and adjust** Regularly check in with ADHD students to ensure their fidget tools remain effective and aren't becoming a source of distraction for themselves or others.

### Teaching tip

Embracing the art of fidgeting requires a shift in perspective. Instead of viewing it as a potential distraction, see it as a lifeline for ADHD students. With the right tools and guidance, fidgeting can be channelled into a productive and beneficial classroom behaviour, enhancing the learning experience for these students.

# IDEA 27

# Body fidgeting

If I'm bouncing my leg or swaying, it's like a rhythm that keeps me tuned in. It might look like I'm not paying attention, but it's the opposite. *Rosa, 15*

**Body fidgeting, from leg bouncing to chair swinging, often serves as a self-regulation tool for many ADHD students. These kinetic behaviours can enhance their concentration, providing sensory feedback that helps anchor their attention.**

### Teaching tip

Body fidgeting is a natural response for many ADHD students, helping them navigate the sensory and cognitive challenges they face. By offering structured movement opportunities and sensory outlets, we can ensure that every student's unique needs are met, fostering an environment where all can thrive.

Here are some strategies you can try:

**Recognise the significance** Understand that body fidgeting is not merely a sign of impatience or boredom. For ADHD students, these movements can be integral to their learning process.

**Provide movement opportunities** Incorporate short breaks where students can stand, stretch or even take a quick walk around the room. This can help ADHD students get the movement they need in structured, non-disruptive ways.

**Flexible seating options** Consider alternatives to traditional seating, like stability balls or wobble stools, which allow for movement while sitting and can be particularly beneficial for ADHD students.

**Educate on boundaries** While fidgeting can be beneficial, it's essential to set boundaries. Teach students to be aware of their movements and ensure they aren't distracting others.

**Engage in sensory activities** Introduce sensory activities which can offer similar benefits to body fidgeting without being as noticeable. For example, stress ball squeezing, playing with feathers or ribbons, or sports bands attached around the front two legs of the chair that they can push their heels back into.

**IDEA 28**

# Toilet breaks

Sometimes, the most mundane requests hide deeper challenges. For our ADHD students, asking for a toilet break during lesson time might be more than just a call of nature. *Mrs. Green, Head of Year*

**Toilet breaks during lesson time, while often seen as a routine request, can carry a more profound significance for ADHD students. From challenges with <u>interoception</u> to the need for movement, understanding the underlying reasons can lead to a more supportive classroom environment.**

Here are some strategies you can try:

**Interoceptive insights** Recognise that many ADHD students, due to co-occurring issues, may struggle with interoception, or the ability to sense internal body signals. This can make it challenging for them to anticipate the need for a toilet break in advance.

**Break-time barriers** Understand that ADHD students might forget or not prioritise using the toilet during breaks, leading to in-class requests. Providing gentle reminders at the beginning of break-time can be beneficial.

**Movement in disguise** Realise that for some ADHD students, asking for a toilet break might be a socially acceptable way of taking a short movement break, helping them to refocus.

**Open communication** Foster an environment where ADHD students feel comfortable discussing their needs. This can help in understanding the frequency of their requests and finding potential solutions.

**Flexible policies** Consider having a flexible policy regarding toilet breaks, understanding the unique challenges ADHD students face. While maintaining classroom discipline, offer them the leeway they might need.

---

**Teaching tip**

Being responsive to the unique needs of ADHD students, even in something as simple as a toilet break request, can make a world of difference. By recognising the challenges they face, from interoception issues to the need for movement, and adapting our approach, we can create a classroom environment that is both structured and supportive, catering to the needs of every student.

## IDEA 29

# Negative self-belief

It's heartbreaking to witness the negative self-perception many of our ADHD students carry. Unravelling years of internalised messages is a challenge, but with understanding and support we can help them rebuild their self-worth. *Ms. Lawrence, SENCO*

**Negative self-belief is a common struggle among ADHD students, rooted in years of perceived failures and external criticisms. Research suggests that by the age of 12, ADHD children might have received 20,000 more negative messages than their peers, leaving an indelible mark on their self-perception.[2]**

### Teaching tip

Building a positive self-belief in ADHD students is a journey that requires persistence, empathy and a lot of positive reinforcement. By recognising the depth of their internal struggles and being a consistent source of encouragement, we can help them reshape their self-perception and embrace their true potential.

Here are some strategies you can try:

**Recognise the weight of the past** Understand the profound impact of the accumulated negative messages on ADHD students' self-belief, which can manifest as self-doubt, hesitation and aversion to trying new things.

**Counteract negative messaging** Introduce consistent positive affirmations and feedback, focusing on their strengths and successes, however small.

**Safe spaces for expression** Create environments where ADHD students can voice their insecurities and negative beliefs, offering validation and understanding.

**Empower through success** Design tasks that allow ADHD students to experience success, boosting their confidence and challenging their negative internal narratives.

**Reframe failures** Teach them that mistakes are opportunities for growth. Help them see failures as learning experiences, not as reflections of their worth.

---

2 Jellinek, M. S. (2010), 'Don't let ADHD crush children's self-esteem.' Clinical Psychiatry News, 38(5), 12.

## IDEA 30

# Negative self-talk

*I always tell myself I should be able to do things like everyone else, but then I fall short and beat myself up about it. It's like a never-ending cycle.* Aiden, 17

**Negative self-talk is not just a series of passing thoughts for ADHD students; it's a constant barrage of self-criticism that can hinder their progress. Coupled with setting <u>neurotypical</u> expectations for themselves, this can lead to a cycle of disappointment and further reinforce their internal criticism.**

Here are some strategies you can try:

**Identify the inner critic** Engage students in conversations to help recognise and label their negative self-talk patterns.

**Challenge and replace** Introduce cognitive-behavioural strategies that challenge negative beliefs and replace them with more positive, realistic affirmations. For example, asking why students feel negatively about themselves, helping them to see that these views are untrue and unhelpful and guiding them towards more positive self-talk.

**Setting realistic expectations** Guide ADHD students in setting expectations based on their unique strengths and challenges, rather than comparing themselves to neurotypical peers.

**Celebrate small victories** Reinforce the importance of acknowledging and celebrating even minor achievements, helping to shift their focus from perceived failures.

**Externalise the critic** Use visual or written exercises to help students externalise their inner critic, making it easier to address and challenge the negative beliefs it perpetuates. For example, ask what they think their friends or teachers would say about them.

### Teaching tip

Supporting ADHD students in navigating their negative self-talk and unrealistic expectations requires patience, understanding and consistent positive reinforcement. By providing them with strategies and tools to challenge their inner critic, we can create a more positive self-view and help them set and achieve realistic goals.

**IDEA 31**

# Emotional dysregulation

*Every emotion our students with ADHD feel is valid. Our role isn't to dismiss or suppress these feelings, but to understand them, validate them, and guide students towards healthier outlets.* Mr. Thompson, Behavioural Specialist

**Emotional dysregulation, manifesting as anger or frustration, is a common challenge for students with ADHD. To effectively support them, we must first validate their feelings and then guide them towards more constructive ways of expressing and managing their emotions.**

### Teaching tip

Validating the emotions of ADHD students is the first and crucial step towards addressing their emotional challenges. By showing understanding and providing tools for healthier expression, we can create a supportive and inclusive learning environment.

Here are some strategies you can try:

**Validate emotions** Begin by acknowledging and validating the student's feelings. Every emotion they experience is real and legitimate.

**Offer understanding** Respond with statements such as, 'I understand why that made you angry. Let's find a way to work through it.'

**Provide calming techniques** Introduce strategies such as deep breathing exercises, short breaks, or quiet spaces to regroup.

**Set clear boundaries** While validating emotions, clarify that certain behaviours are not acceptable and discuss alternative ways to express feelings.

**Open channels of communication** Encourage students to communicate their feelings and frustrations, ensuring they feel understood.

**Collaborate on solutions** Engage the student in identifying strategies that work for them, giving them a sense of ownership over their emotional responses.

**Educate peers** Foster an understanding environment by educating classmates about ADHD and wider neurodiversity, promoting empathy and support.

**Reflect and adjust** Continually evaluate the effectiveness of strategies and adjust based on the student's needs and feedback.

# IDEA 32

# Emotional overwhelm

It's essential to see beyond the tears and understand the depth of emotions our ADHD students might be feeling. What may seem like an overreaction to us can be a genuine emotional response for them.
*Ms. Patel, School Counsellor*

**For students with ADHD, emotional responses can often be intense, leading to bouts of tears and profound sadness that may seem disproportionate to the situation. Recognising the validity and depth of these emotions is crucial in offering effective support and understanding.**

Here are some strategies you can try:

**Acknowledge the emotion** Always begin by recognising and validating the student's feelings, understanding that their emotional intensity is real for them.

**Seek understanding** Instead of dismissing the tears, ask open-ended questions to understand the root of their emotions better.

**Set boundaries with compassion** While it's essential to validate emotions, it's equally vital to guide students in understanding the appropriateness of their reactions in different situations.

**Encourage emotional expression** Help students identify healthier outlets for their emotions, such as journaling, art or talking it out.

**Collaborate on coping strategies** Engage the student in developing personal coping techniques that resonate with them.

**Seek specialist support** Consider seeking the expertise of school counsellors or therapists to provide additional support and coping tools.

**Reflect and adjust** Continuously monitor and adjust strategies based on the student's evolving emotional needs and feedback.

> **Teaching tip**
>
> Emotions, especially in ADHD students, can be vast and overwhelming. Our role is to validate, understand and guide them through these intense moments, ensuring they feel supported every step of the way.

# IDEA 33

# Friendships

I want to be close to people, but sometimes I either come on too strong or drift away without meaning to. It's like I can't find the right balance. *Sienna, 15*

**The realm of friendships presents unique challenges for ADHD students, with ADHD characteristics often impacting social dynamics. While they have so much to offer in friendships, finding equilibrium and a sense of belonging can be an intricate journey.**

Here are some strategies you can try:

**Acknowledge the differences** Recognise and celebrate the unique traits ADHD students bring to friendships, such as creativity, energy and a fresh perspective.

**Teach balance** Provide guidance on understanding the fine line between hyper-focusing on a friend and unintentionally neglecting them.

**Emotional regulation support** Help students manage their emotional responses, to prevent impulsive reactions that might strain friendships (see **Idea 31**).

**Promote inclusion** Create classroom activities that foster inclusivity, allowing ADHD students to feel part of the group, such as an activity where the class write positive statements about each other, and what they value about them.

**Social skills training** Offer opportunities for ADHD students to learn and practise essential social skills in a safe environment.

**Encourage reflection** Allow students to reflect on their interactions, helping them to understand and learn from social successes and missteps.

**Build resilience** Teach students that every individual faces challenges in friendships and that setbacks can be opportunities for growth and learning.

---

**Bonus idea** ★

Initiate a 'Friendship Mentor' programme in school, where peers support each other in navigating the complexities of social relationships, providing a safe space for ADHD students to express their feelings and seek guidance.

# Classroom management

# IDEA 34

# Off-task shouting and tangents

Sometimes, I just think of something cool and want to share it. *Jake, 14*

**Students with ADHD can occasionally shout out or divert the class with tangents that seem relevant or intriguing to them. These tangents can be genuine distractions or, at times, deliberate deflections, especially when faced with unfamiliar teaching settings.**

### Teaching tip

Remember that for ADHD students, these tangents or off-topic comments can often stem from a place of genuine curiosity or, at times, a need for dopamine-driven stimulation. While it's essential to manage these diversions for the sake of the class, it's equally crucial to do so with understanding and empathy. Over time, by fostering a supportive and structured environment, students can learn to better manage their impulses and remain on topic.

Here are some strategies you can try:

**Empathetic acknowledgement** Recognise the student's contribution without dismissing it, but steer them back to the topic. A simple, 'That's an interesting thought, Jake, let's discuss it later,' can work wonders.

**Establish clear boundaries** Set clear expectations about classroom decorum, especially during discussions. Reinforce the importance of staying on topic.

**Private check-ins** If a student frequently goes off on tangents, take a moment after class to chat with them. Understand their perspective and provide guidance.

**Be prepared for deflections** Especially with substitute or less familiar teachers, ADHD students might use tangents as a form of entertainment. It's essential to be aware of this and not get drawn into prolonged off-topic discussions.

**Engage with relevance** Make lessons engaging and relevant to reduce the likelihood of students seeking external stimuli.

**Use visual aids** A clear agenda or roadmap of the lesson can help students see where the class is headed and reduce the temptation to divert the discussion.

# IDEA 35

# Not shouting out

They're excited that they know the answer. *Ms. Yentis, Geography Teacher*

**Children with ADHD often shout out answers impulsively in class, driven by a combination of excitement, a desire to be the first, and challenges with working memory. Understanding the underlying reasons can guide teachers in fostering a classroom environment where all students feel valued and heard.**

Here are some strategies you can try:

**Acknowledge and redirect** If a student with ADHD shouts out an answer, acknowledge it (especially if it's correct) but gently remind them of classroom etiquette and the importance of giving everyone a chance.

**Understanding natural consequences** If the shouted-out answer is incorrect, refrain from harsh reprimands. The discomfort of being wrong can be lesson enough.

**Implement take-up time** Counting down from five with a visual aid, such as fingers, provides a clear structure for students to prepare and reduces impulsive outbursts.

**Encourage writing it down** Equip students with whiteboards, sticky notes or a space in their book to jot down answers. This reduces impulsiveness and provides a concrete way for them to engage with the material.

**Repetition is key** If revisiting a student for their answer, always repeat the question. This accounts for their working memory challenges and ensures they aren't caught off guard.

**Promote equity** Stress the importance of every student having an opportunity to think and answer, reinforcing the value of patience and turn-taking.

### Teaching tip

Fostering active learning in students with ADHD is crucial. Embrace their enthusiasm but ensure it's channelled in a constructive way that doesn't add stress or urgency. This involves setting clear expectations, while also being understanding of their unique challenges. Over time, with consistent reinforcement, these students can remain actively engaged in learning, while adhering to classroom norms.

**IDEA 36**

# Classroom distractions

Whenever someone asks a question, whispers to a friend, or even opens the door, my attention zips to it. It's like I'm trying to watch a movie, but someone keeps changing the channel. *Layla, 12*

**The dynamic nature of classrooms, with their spontaneous interactions and unpredictable moments, can create a whirlwind of distractions for ADHD students. From peers' actions to unexpected interruptions, these elements can significantly divert their focus, underscoring the need for tailored support strategies.**

Here are some strategies you can try:

**Set classroom norms** Establish clear guidelines about unnecessary chatter, random movements, and respecting peers' focus, creating a more conducive environment for all.

**Minimise door interruptions** Whenever feasible, limit non-essential interruptions by coordinating with other staff members about timings for entering or passing messages.

**Noise-cancelling tools** Consider allowing ADHD students the use of noise-cancelling headphones or earplugs during independent work sessions.

**Proactive engagement** Keep lessons interactive and engaging, capturing ADHD students' attention and reducing the likelihood of their minds wandering.

**Peer awareness** Conduct short sessions educating peers about ADHD and the challenges of distractions, fostering a more empathetic and supportive classroom community.

> **Teaching tip**
>
> Understanding the unique challenges ADHD students face in bustling classrooms is essential. While we can't control every variable, through proactive measures and cultivating awareness we can significantly reduce distractions. In doing so, we create a more inclusive environment where ADHD students can navigate their learning with fewer hurdles.

# IDEA 37

# Back to work after a distraction

Distractions are a part of life, especially in the classroom. But for our ADHD students, the journey back to the task post-distraction often requires gentle signposting and understanding. *Mrs. Clarke, Learning Support Assistant*

**Every student faces distractions, but for those with ADHD, returning to the task at hand can be particularly challenging. With the right strategies and a compassionate approach, teachers can effectively guide these students back on track without causing undue stress.**

Here are some strategies you can try:

**No recrimination** Approach the distracted student with empathy and understanding, avoiding any tone of blame or reprimand.

**Scaffolded support** Offer cues or prompts to help the student pick up where they left off. This can be a quick recap, a question about the last thing they remember, or pointing to a specific line or problem.

**Signalling** Use non-verbal cues to gently redirect the student's attention. A double tap on their desk or using their name followed by a double tap on your forearm can serve as subtle, non-disruptive reminders.

**Visual aids** Consider using visual aids, like bookmarks or sticky notes, to help students quickly identify where they left off.

**Structured breaks** Recognise that everyone, especially ADHD students, benefits from short, planned breaks. This can help reset their focus and reduce the impact of distractions.

### Teaching tip

Guiding ADHD students back to task after distractions is as much about the 'how' as the 'what'. The key is to offer support without making them feel singled out or criticised. By creating a classroom environment of understanding and patience, you pave the way for these students to bounce back from distractions with resilience and confidence.

# IDEA 38

# Inclusive seating plans

Every student has a spot where they shine brightest in the classroom. For our ADHD students, finding this place is crucial, as it can significantly enhance their engagement and learning experience.
*Mr. Ahmed, Behavioural Specialist*

**An inclusive seating plan is about more than just organisation; it's a strategic tool that sets the stage for optimal learning. For ADHD students, the right seating arrangement can make a tangible difference, providing them with an environment where they can harness their strengths and minimise distractions.**

### Teaching tip

Where young people sit matters to them, and while you will generally be thinking about where everyone works best, other factors might be at play. Feelings of psychological safety are a pre-requisite to any learning, so if a student is displaying an overt or unusual reaction to your seating plan, consider who or what your plan places them close to, or far away from.

Here are some strategies you can try:

**Open dialogue** Engage with the ADHD student to understand their preferences and needs. Involving them in the seating decision fosters a sense of ownership and collaboration.

**Trial and error** Be flexible and open to adjustments. What's effective for one ADHD student might not be for another. Periodically reassess seating arrangements to ensure they're still beneficial.

**Consider surroundings** Take into account the classroom's sensory stimuli, like lighting and noise levels, and place ADHD students in spots where these are least disruptive to them.

**Group dynamics** Think about the personalities and learning styles of neighbouring students. Strategic pairings can be beneficial for collaborative work and mutual support.

**Clear boundaries** While flexibility is essential, it's equally vital to set clear boundaries. Ensure that every student knows the classroom expectations, regardless of where they're seated.

# IDEA 39

# Classroom chatter

*In every classroom, there's a hum of conversation. But for our ADHD students, this chatter isn't just background noise; it's a way of processing and engaging. Our challenge is to harness it productively.*
*Mrs. Collins, Year Group Leader*

**Classroom chatter is a natural part of the learning environment, but for ADHD students it holds a unique significance. While talking can aid their understanding and boost dopamine levels, it's essential to strike a balance so that it benefits their learning without disrupting the class.**

Here are some strategies you can try:

**Structured discussions** Incorporate regular group discussions or peer-sharing moments into lessons, giving ADHD students an outlet to process information verbally.

**Set clear boundaries** While it's essential to allow some degree of chatter, set clear expectations about when it's appropriate to talk and when it's time to listen.

**Silent signals** Introduce non-verbal cues, such as raising a hand or a visual card system, to help students identify when they might be veering into disruptive territory.

**Peer partners** Pair ADHD students with understanding classmates who can help guide discussions back to the topic if they begin to stray. This comes with a risk of putting a burden on the classmate; to mitigate this, make it clear that each student retains responsibility for their own learning and self-control.

**Reflection time** Dedicate a few minutes post-discussion for students, especially those with ADHD, to jot down their thoughts, solidifying their understanding.

### Teaching tip

Embracing the chatter of ADHD students requires understanding and strategy. It's not about stifling their need to talk but about channelling it in ways that enhance their learning experience and maintain a productive classroom environment. Through structured discussions and clear boundaries, every student can find their voice without overshadowing others.

### Taking it further

A phrase I often use is: 'If you want the right to talk, you have the responsibility to stay in control, keep it on task, and stop when it is time to move on.' This tends to resonate and give a set boundary and expectation. Remember that you are looking for better, not perfect.

# IDEA 40

# Low-level disruptive talking

I don't always realise I'm talking or disrupting. Sometimes, my thoughts just spill out, and other times I just need a quick chat to process what's happening. *Mia, 16*

**Low-level disruptive talking is a challenge many teachers face, especially when catering to the needs of ADHD students. Differentiating between unintentional and intentional disruptions is key to addressing the issue and maintaining a focused classroom environment.**

### Teaching tip

Low-level disruptive talking, especially among ADHD students, can be a symptom of their need for stimulation or a result of their rapid thought processes. Addressing this requires a blend of understanding, clear boundaries and proactive strategies. By creating a classroom environment that acknowledges their needs while maintaining discipline, you can ensure a harmonious and productive learning space for all.

Here are some strategies you can try:

**Active intervention** Address unintentional disruptions promptly but gently, making the ADHD student aware without causing embarrassment.

**Clear expectations** At the start of the lesson, set clear expectations about talking and disruptions. Reinforce these rules as needed, ensuring they are understood by all.

**Non-verbal cues** Develop silent signals, like a hand gesture or a visual card, to alert students when they're being disruptive, allowing them to self-correct without drawing too much attention.

**Structured breaks** Incorporate short breaks or interactive segments into the lesson, giving students, especially those with ADHD, a chance to talk and refocus.

**Peer feedback** Encourage students to gently remind each other to stay on track, fostering a collaborative and supportive classroom culture.

## IDEA 41

# Unintended distractions

In every classroom, there's a rhythm, a flow that drives the learning process. But for our ADHD students, their natural impulses, be it fidgeting, tapping or chatting, can unintentionally disrupt this flow for others. *Ms. Patterson, Head of Inclusion*

**Every student brings their own set of behaviours to the classroom, but for ADHD students, their involuntary actions can sometimes lead to unintended distractions. While these behaviours are often a coping mechanism or a way to self-regulate, they can pose challenges in a classroom setting.**

Here are some strategies you can try:

**Open communication** Discuss the behaviours with the ADHD student privately, ensuring they understand how their actions might impact others and exploring alternative ways to self-regulate.

**Provide fidget tools** Offer ADHD students discreet fidget tools, such as stress balls, spiral hair bands or the prickly side of sticky backed hook and loop attached to the underside of the desk, that allow them to channel their need for movement without causing disruptions.

**Structured movement breaks** Incorporate short movement breaks into the lesson, giving all students a chance to stretch and refocus, thereby reducing the impulse to fidget.

**Noise awareness** Educate the class about noise levels, and encourage students to be mindful of unintentional noises, such as pen clicking or tapping.

**Seating arrangements** Consider placing ADHD students in areas where their movements will be less likely to distract others, while still ensuring they are engaged with the lesson.

### Teaching tip

Understanding the 'why' behind ADHD students' involuntary actions is crucial. They aren't trying to be disruptive; they're simply trying to navigate their own unique challenges. By providing them with tools, strategies and understanding, you create an inclusive environment where every student feels valued and understood, while also maintaining a productive classroom dynamic.

# IDEA 42

# Deliberate distractions

Sometimes, students with ADHD will act out, not out of malice, but in search of something that makes them feel more alert and engaged. It's our job to understand the 'why' behind these actions and find ways to channel their energy positively. *Mr. Dawson, Educational Psychologist*

**For ADHD students, especially those with hyperactive tendencies, the classroom can sometimes feel like a balancing act between under-stimulation and over-stimulation. This can lead to deliberate distractions as they chase the dopamine rush to regulate their feelings, a phenomenon I have named 'the great dopamine chase'.**

### Teaching tip

The great dopamine chase is a reality for many ADHD students, driving them to seek engagement and stimulation in ways that can disrupt the learning environment. However, by recognising the underlying causes and providing positive, constructive outlets, you can help them navigate their needs while maintaining classroom harmony. It's all about understanding, empathy and strategic intervention.

Here are some strategies you can try:

**Recognise the chase** Understand that when ADHD students deliberately distract others, they are often seeking a dopamine boost to either increase alertness or manage overwhelming feelings.

**Engaging content** Ensure lessons are interactive and stimulating, reducing the need for students to seek external sources of engagement.

**Provide constructive outlets** Offer structured ways for students to get their dopamine fix, such as short, engaging tasks or challenges that capture their attention.

**Open dialogue** Talk to the student about their actions, ensuring they understand the impact on others and exploring alternative ways to meet their needs.

**Positive reinforcements** Subtly acknowledge ADHD students when they channel their energy into constructive tasks, reinforcing the idea that there are positive ways to get the stimulation they seek. A nod of approval is a great source of dopamine.

**IDEA 43**

# Attention-seeking behaviours

I don't always know how to ask for what I need, so sometimes I act out. It's not that I want to be the centre of attention, I just want to feel connected. *Aisha, 13*

**Attention-seeking behaviours, often observed in ADHD students, can be misconstrued as mere disruptions. In reality, these actions frequently stem from a deeper desire for connection, understanding and validation.**

Here are some strategies you can try:

**Empathetic observation** Recognise that behind every attention-seeking behaviour is an unmet need. Observe and try to understand what the ADHD student is truly seeking.

**Open channels of communication** Foster an environment where students feel comfortable expressing their feelings, concerns and needs. Regular check-ins can help in understanding their motivations.

**Positive affirmation** Reinforce good behaviours and achievements, offering ADHD students the positive attention they might be seeking. This can redirect their need for attention to more constructive avenues.

**Peer support** Encourage classmates to be understanding and supportive. A buddy system or mentoring can help ADHD students feel connected and understood.

**Structured interventions** Offer structured activities or roles in the classroom that allow ADHD students to gain positive attention, such as being a group leader or helper.

### Teaching tip

Attention-seeking behaviours in ADHD students are often less about the 'attention' and more about the 'seeking'. They seek understanding, connection and affirmation. By shifting our perspective from disruption to connection-seeking, we can address the root causes and guide these students towards positive interactions and self-affirmation.

# IDEA 44

# Low-dopamine attention-seeking

Attention-seeking isn't always about the spotlight; for our ADHD students, it's often a quest for a dopamine boost. Recognising this can reshape how we respond and support. *Dr. Lewis, School Counsellor*

**Attention-seeking behaviours in ADHD students can often be traced back to their neurochemical needs, particularly the pursuit of dopamine. This chase, previously explored as 'the great dopamine chase', extends to various behaviours, with attention-seeking being a prominent manifestation.**

> **Teaching tip**
>
> Understanding the neurochemical needs of ADHD students reframes how we view attention-seeking behaviours. It's not merely a bid for the spotlight, but a neurochemical quest for balance. By providing consistent, positive attention and engaging learning experiences, we can help ADHD students find the balance they seek without resorting to disruptive behaviours.

Here are some strategies you can try:

**Recognise the underlying need** Understand that attention-seeking behaviours are often an attempt to elevate dopamine levels. It's less about the attention itself and more about the feeling it induces.

**Revisit Idea 42** Reflect on strategies that address deliberate distractions, as these can also apply to attention-seeking behaviours. The core principle is to offer alternative sources of dopamine boosts.

**Affirmation and validation** Provide ADHD students with regular positive feedback. Recognising their efforts offers a dopamine boost in a constructive way.

**Engage and involve** Incorporate interactive and stimulating activities in lessons. Engaging tasks can naturally elevate dopamine levels, reducing the need for external attention-seeking behaviours.

**Consistent check-ins** Regularly connect with ADHD students, ensuring they feel seen and understood. These moments of connection can satiate their need for attention in positive ways.

**IDEA 45**

# Pushing boundaries

When ADHD students push the buttons of their peers, it's often a complex interplay of seeking stimulation, asserting control, or even finding amusement. Our role is to delve deeper into these motivations and guide them towards healthier interactions.
*Mrs. Patel, School Counsellor*

**For some ADHD students, pushing the boundaries and eliciting reactions from peers can be a manifestation of their condition's complexities. Whether driven by a need for stimulation, a bid for control, or simple amusement, understanding the root causes can pave the way for better interpersonal dynamics.**

Here are some strategies you can try:

**Unearth the underlying motives** Recognise that button-pushing behaviours in ADHD students might stem from their need for stimulation, control or even amusement.

**Open dialogue** Engage ADHD students in conversations about their actions, helping them reflect on the impact on others and the reasons behind their behaviours.

**Provide constructive outlets** Offer ADHD students structured activities or roles in the classroom that allow them to gain positive attention and meet their need for stimulation in constructive ways.

**Teach empathy** Incorporate lessons and discussions around empathy, helping ADHD students understand the feelings and perspectives of their peers.

**Conflict resolution** When conflicts arise from button-pushing behaviours, provide a platform for open communication and resolution between the involved parties.

### Teaching tip

Understanding the button-pushing behaviours of ADHD students requires us to delve into their deeper motivations. By offering them positive avenues for stimulation and teaching them the value of empathy, we can guide them towards healthier interactions that enrich the classroom environment for everyone.

### Taking it further

When peers provoke ADHD students, aware of their vulnerabilities, it's crucial to explore the peer's intentions and make it clear such behaviour is unkind and unacceptable. Teachers should set expectations for respect and understanding, guiding all towards empathy and positive classroom interactions.

# Distractions, disruptions and disrespect

Part 5

## IDEA 46

# Disrespectful conduct

When faced with a defiant student, it's crucial to ponder: Have we inadvertently shown disrespect, prompting this reaction?
*Mr. Thompson, Pastoral Lead*

**In the intricate dance of classroom dynamics, both educators and students can sometimes miss a step, leading to mutual feelings of disrespect. For students with ADHD, this misstep can be particularly challenging, as they often grapple with impulsivity and perceptions of fairness.**

### Teaching tip
Host regular classroom feedback sessions, allowing students to express their feelings about the class environment, thereby creating a mutual understanding and fostering a shared ethos of respect. This proactive approach can help anticipate and mitigate potential conflicts.

Here are some strategies you can try:

**Recognise and reflect** Educators should continually evaluate their behaviour and communication, ensuring they're not conveying unintended disrespect.

**Open channels of communication** Facilitate spaces where students can voice feelings of disrespect, and educators can transparently share their viewpoints.

**Ensure fair discipline** Implement disciplinary actions that are just, consistent and explained in ways students can comprehend.

**Champion empathy and active listening** Urge both educators and students to listen attentively, aiming to truly grasp the other's viewpoint.

**Embrace restorative practices** Shift from mere punitive measures to practices centred on mending and understanding, tackling the core causes of disrespect.

# IDEA 47

# Rule adherence

I'm not trying to be sassy. Some of the rules just seem ridiculous and impossible. *Lara, 14*

**For many educators, setting and enforcing rules is a staple, but for students with ADHD, understanding and adhering can be a labyrinth. To navigate this maze, it's crucial for educators to fathom the underlying challenges and tailor supportive responses.**

Here are some strategies you can try:

**Identify sensory triggers** Recognise that rules related to sensory stimuli might be challenging for some students.

**Acknowledge impulsivity** Understand that ADHD students might act without considering rule implications due to inherent impulsiveness.

**Clarify rules** Ensure rules and their reasons are communicated lucidly, aiding in understanding and compliance.

**Adopt flexibility** Adapt rules when necessary, appreciating that individual needs may vary.

**Maintain consistent outcomes** Ensure consequences are consistent and focus on educating, not just reprimanding.

**Promote positive behaviour** Prioritise recognising and rewarding rule adherence to encourage repeated positive actions.

**Rule reflection** Consider creating a 'Rule Reflection' session where students can discuss and understand classroom rules, allowing a space for concerns to be voiced and addressed. This proactive approach can reduce rule-related confrontations.

> **Bonus idea** ★
>
> Encourage students to help devise classroom rules, giving them agency and fostering a sense of belonging. This collaborative effort aids adherence and understanding, as well as building a supportive environment where every student, including those with ADHD, feels valued and integral to the classroom community.

## IDEA 48

# Low-level persistent disruption

Those little disruptions, while seeming minor, can snowball into bigger challenges. We must understand the 'why' behind them to navigate effectively. *Mr. Williams, Year 9 Form Tutor*

**Low-level persistent disruption (LLPD)** might appear as minor classroom interruptions, but can gradually erode the lesson's structure. For ADHD students, these disruptions are less about defiance and more a reflection of their unique neurodiversity.

Here are some strategies you can try:

**Recognise the unintentional** Understand that ADHD-driven behaviours, like constant tapping or spontaneous outbursts, contribute to LLPD.

**Avoid the behaviour points trap** Ensure that ADHD students aren't unfairly penalised for their innate behaviours, which could demoralise them further.

**Address the 'pressure cooker' effect** Prevent the accumulation of stress by recognising and addressing the root causes of LLPD.

**Challenge labelling and its effects** Steer clear of labelling students based on prior exclusions or sanctions, as it affects their self-perception and peer relationships. They need and deserve a fresh start, and you model the behaviour and attitude that other students might emulate.

**Bridge the academic gaps** If there are gaps in learning, there needs to be a plan and resources in place to help with this. Providing information and resources, as well as understanding the psychological impact, is important, and shows the student that they matter to you.

**Empower through engagement** Instead of purely enforcing rules, involve ADHD students in discussions and solution finding, fostering ownership and self-regulation.

### Teaching tip

'Reasonable adjustments' are implemented to provide neurodivergent children with a level playing field, but come into conflict with zero tolerance behaviour policies. They spotlight neurodivergent children as deviations from the 'norm', which not only stigmatises them but also misses the point: true inclusivity lies in designing systems that recognise and respect neurodiversity, rather than making after-the-fact adjustments.

### Bonus idea ★

Introduce 'Classroom Contracts', where students collaboratively decide on classroom norms, promoting a sense of ownership and reducing chances of LLPD. This can foster understanding and mutual respect among peers.

# IDEA 49

# 'Answering back' behaviour

*ADHD students aren't answering back just to be defiant; they're often processing emotions, seeking justice, and reflecting what they perceive. It's our job to understand and guide this response.*
*Ms. Harper, Behavioural Specialist*

**The behaviour of 'answering back' in ADHD students can often be a manifestation of various underlying factors, from emotional dysregulation to a heightened sense of justice. Understanding these triggers can help educators navigate and address these responses more effectively.**

Here are some strategies you can try:

**Emotional waves** Recognise that ADHD students can experience intense emotional dysregulation, making them more reactive and leading to spontaneous responses.

**Justice and fairness** Understand their heightened sense of justice, which can make them vocal when they perceive something as unfair or unjust, even if that perception differs from reality.

**Mirroring perceived attitudes** ADHD students often mirror the attitude they believe they're receiving. Maintain a calm and neutral tone, ensuring they don't feel attacked or defensive.

**The 'why' factor** Much like their need to understand tasks, ADHD students often need clarity on decisions or actions that involve them. This need can lead to questioning that might come off as 'answering back'.

**Guiding impulse control** Help ADHD students develop better impulse control, allowing them to think before they react, using more constructive responses. It is common for ADHDers to feel an imperative to correct what they perceive as 'wrong' in others, and it is important to correct this instinct, developing the option to let things go, or respond, rather than being reactive.

### Teaching tip

Engaging with an ADHD student who frequently 'answers back' requires a blend of empathy, patience and strategic intervention. By understanding the myriad factors driving this behaviour and providing them with tools and understanding, we can transform these interactions into learning opportunities, fostering better communication and mutual respect.

# IDEA 50

# Oppositional behaviour

I don't want to be difficult, but sometimes it feels like everything's against me, and I just need to push back. *Layla, 14*

**Oppositional behaviour in ADHD students often stems from deeper challenges than mere rebelliousness. To effectively navigate this behaviour, educators must understand its roots in emotional dysregulation, a heightened sense of justice, perceived attitudes and impulse control challenges.**

### Teaching tip

When addressing **oppositional defiant disorder (ODD)**, teachers should offer consistent, non-confrontational support. By not taking behaviours personally, lowering demands during escalated moments, and providing a safe space, educators can help ODD students feel secure and understood, fostering a calmer classroom atmosphere.

Here are some strategies you can try:

**Understand emotional turmoil** Recognise that the emotional intensity often felt by ADHD students can result in oppositional behaviour. This reaction is less about defiance and more about self-preservation.

**Justice on the frontline** A heightened sense of justice can make ADHD students more vocal and resistant when they perceive unfair treatment, even if their perception doesn't align with reality.

**Reflecting perceived attitudes** ADHD students might display oppositional behaviour as a reflection of the attitude or treatment they believe they're receiving. Maintaining a calm, consistent approach can help in diffusing potential confrontations.

**Seeking clarity** Their inherent need to understand 'why' can be mistaken for opposition. Providing clear rationales and involving them in decision-making can mitigate this.

**Building impulse control** Continuous guidance to help them develop impulse control can be beneficial. 'Stop, Think, Do' is an intervention that helps develop moments to pause before action. It helps teachers to say 'stop' rather than shouting, and the student understands that this isn't a judgement, it an opportunity to pause and think before they act.[3]

---

[3] www.stopthinkdo.com

**IDEA 51**

# Self-opposition

I know what I should do, and I want to do it. But there are times when it feels like there's a wall inside me, stopping me. *Nathan, 15*

**For ADHD students, self-opposition can be a perplexing challenge. They might grapple with an internal resistance that prevents them from doing tasks or following through, even when they genuinely want to.**

Here are some strategies you can try:

**Recognise the inner struggle** Understand that ADHD students often face a conflict between their intentions and their ability to execute them. This struggle isn't about laziness or defiance but a genuine internal barrier.

**Neurological barriers** Be aware that the ADHD brain's neurochemistry, particularly dopamine pathways, can sometimes create a resistance to starting or completing tasks, even desired ones.

**Emotional overwhelm** Emotional dysregulation can lead to feelings of overwhelm, making tasks seem insurmountable and leading to self-opposition.

**Build self-awareness** Help students identify and articulate when they're feeling this inner resistance. Giving a name to the feeling can be the first step in addressing it.

**Strategies for overcoming** Introduce techniques like breaking tasks into smaller steps, using positive self-talk, and leveraging external motivators to help ADHD students overcome their self-opposition. For example, if they want to be a teacher in future, but struggle with maths revision, remind them of their end goal to make the revision purposeful.

### Teaching tip

Supporting ADHD students through their internal battles requires patience, understanding, and a toolbox of strategies. Recognising that they're often fighting against their own brain's wiring, and not their intentions, can shift the perspective and open the door to more effective interventions and support.

# IDEA 52

# Anxiety

It feels like my brain is always on alert, even when there's no real danger. I know it's trying to protect me, but it just ends up making things harder. *Sam, 15*

**While anxiety inherently serves as a protective mechanism, alerting us to potential threats based on past experiences, it can become maladaptive in ADHD students. Instead of being a beneficial warning system, it can escalate into a chronic state of heightened alertness, often disproportionate to the actual threat.**

Here are some strategies you can try:

**Understand the origin** Recognise that anxiety's primary function is to protect by alerting us to potential dangers based on prior experiences.

**Identifying overreactions** Help ADHD students differentiate between constructive anxiety responses and maladaptive overreactions, allowing them to better gauge when their anxiety is disproportionate.

**Open conversations** Encourage students to share anxieties, helping them process their feelings, and discerning between genuine concerns and unwarranted fears.

**Strategies for balance** Introduce techniques to help manage anxiety responses, such as CBT approaches, grounding exercises or mindfulness practices. Anxiety can be helpful to learn from past mistakes but it can become a problem if it makes it hard to carry out everyday tasks. Encourage students to understand their relationship with their anxiety, rather than feeling like it shouldn't be there at all.

**Empowerment and control** Ways to actively manage anxiety range from recognising triggers to implementing coping mechanisms. For example, ADHD students can try journaling to understand and then limit exposure to their triggers in class.

---

### Teaching tip

Lean into cognitive-behavioural strategies and mindfulness practices, acknowledging that while anxiety can be a helpful alert system, it can become maladaptive (go too far) if it impedes important activities. Equip ADHD students with tools such as deep breathing, guided visualisation and positive self-talk to manage anxiety and enhance focus in the classroom.

# Memory

# Part 6

# IDEA 53

# Working memory challenges: a mental arithmetic example

ADHD isn't about not knowing the answer; it's often about not being able to hold on to the answer long enough to use it. *Mr. Callum, Maths Teacher*

**Students with ADHD frequently grapple with working memory challenges, which can significantly impede their academic progress, particularly in subjects that require mental processing, such as mathematics. One stark example of this is the struggle faced by these students in mental arithmetic tasks, where holding multiple pieces of information simultaneously is key.**

#### Teaching tip

Understanding the nature of working memory challenges in ADHD students is crucial. It's not a lack of understanding or intelligence but a difficulty in holding and manipulating information mentally. Being patient, offering repeated explanations when necessary, and providing strategies to support working memory can make a world of difference in their learning journey.

Here are some strategies you can try:

**Chunking information** Break down problems into smaller steps, allowing students to tackle one piece at a time without feeling overwhelmed.

**Visual aids** Use number lines, counters or written methods to support mental arithmetic. Visual representation can offload the working memory.

**Repetition and practice** Regular practice can help embed processes, reducing the working memory load over time.

**Encourage note-taking** Allow students to jot down intermediary steps or results to prevent forgetting them as they progress. Make this normal in your classroom.

**Use of mnemonics** Teach memory aids or rhymes that can assist in remembering steps or formulas.

**Interactive teaching** Engage students in discussions, group activities or interactive platforms that reinforce learning and make it more tangible.

# IDEA 54

# Working memory challenges: multitasking for written tasks

When I write, it feels like I'm playing a game of Whack-a-Mole. As soon as I focus on one thing, another pops up! *Rahul, 16*

**When it comes to written tasks, ADHD students often find themselves overwhelmed by the multiple elements they need to focus on simultaneously. Balancing handwriting, spelling, punctuation, grammar (SPaG) and content can be a Herculean task due to the working memory challenges associated with ADHD.**

Here are some strategies you can try:

**Drafting** Encourage first drafts that focus solely on content, allowing students to get their ideas down without worrying about SPaG.

**Segmented revision** Once the content is down, guide students to revise one aspect at a time – first spelling, then punctuation, then grammar.

**Handwriting practice** Consider separate sessions or tools focused on improving handwriting without the pressure of content creation.

**Use of technology** Introduce tools like spell checkers or voice-to-text software to help reduce the multitasking load.

**Visual aids** Provide checklists or mnemonic devices to help students remember key SPaG rules.

**Peer review** Encourage peer editing sessions, where students can focus on providing feedback for one aspect at a time, aiding their own understanding in the process.

> **Bonus idea** ★
>
> Consider using coloured pencils or highlighters during the editing process. For instance, students can use one colour for spelling corrections, another for punctuation, and so on. This not only makes the process more interactive but also provides a visual representation of areas that might need more focus.

# IDEA 55

# Short-term memory

I often feel like I've walked into a room and forgotten why. That's how it feels with short-term memory challenges. *Ella, 15*

**Short-term memory acts as a temporary storage for information, holding onto it just long enough to be used or transferred to long-term storage. For students with ADHD, this fleeting memory store can sometimes be even more transient, making certain learning tasks particularly challenging.**

Here are some strategies you can try:

**Repetition is key** Reinforce information through repetition, allowing it to be consolidated in the student's mind.

**Chunking** Break down information into smaller, more manageable chunks to aid retention.

**Visual aids** Incorporate charts, diagrams and other visual tools to provide a visual snapshot of the information.

**Interactive learning** Engage students in discussions, quizzes and interactive activities that require them to recall and use the information immediately.

**Mnemonic devices** Teach students mnemonic techniques that can help in **encoding** information more effectively.

**Immediate application** Encourage students to use new information or skills right away, helping to reinforce their memory.

**Consistent review** Regularly revisit previously taught material to refresh students' memories and strengthen retention.

### Teaching tip

Remember that everyone forgets, but for ADHD students, that forgetfulness can feel more frequent and frustrating. Be patient and provide multiple opportunities for recall. Celebrate successes, no matter how small, to build confidence and positive associations with learning.

**IDEA 56**

# Long-term memory

With ADHD students, once something clicks and gets stored in their long-term memory, it's there for good. It's like they have a vault where certain experiences and learnings are securely locked away.
*Ms. Hughes, History Teacher*

**Long-term memory in students with ADHD can be both a powerful asset and a puzzling challenge. While they often demonstrate an impressive ability to retain certain patterns, skills and experiences, other memories might seem distant or inaccessible due to their present-focused mindset.**

Here are some strategies you can try:

**Relevance is crucial** Make learning material meaningful and relatable for ADHD students, increasing the likelihood of it being stored long-term.

**Consistent application** Encourage the repeated use of newly acquired skills to strengthen their imprint in long-term memory.

**Emotional connection** Memories tied to emotions are often more vividly retained. Engage students emotionally in the learning process.

**Storytelling** Convert information into narratives or stories, making it more memorable and easier to recall.

**Active reflection** Regularly prompt students to reflect on past experiences and lessons, reinforcing their long-term recall.

**Mind mapping** Visual representations like mind maps can help in connecting and consolidating information, facilitating long-term storage.

**Celebrate milestones** Create punctuating moments in the learning journey through celebrations, achievements and recognitions.

> **Teaching tip**
>
> Understanding the nuances of ADHD students' long-term memory can be the key to unlocking their potential. Embrace their strengths and provide support where needed. Remember that every student's memory landscape is unique, and a personalised approach can work wonders.

## IDEA 57

# The challenge of recall

It's like the information is there in my brain, but sometimes I just can't find the key to unlock it, especially when I'm stressed. *Aisha, 15*

**Recall challenges can be particularly daunting for students with ADHD, especially during high-pressure situations like exams. While they may have a vast reservoir of information, accessing it promptly and effectively can sometimes be a hurdle.**

Here are some strategies you can try:

**Visual memory boost** Encourage students to associate information with images, diagrams or mind maps. This visual cue can often trigger recall more effectively than rote memorisation.

**Chunking information** Break down complex data into smaller, more digestible chunks. This reduces the cognitive load during recall.

**Mnemonic devices** Use mnemonic devices, rhymes or acronyms to aid in remembering specific pieces of information or sequences.

**Practice under pressure** Simulate exam conditions during revision sessions to acclimatise students to the pressure and improve recall during actual exams.

**Systematic and frequent recall** The more often information is revisited, the stronger the **neural pathways** become.

**Mindful breathing** Teach students deep breathing techniques. A few moments of focused breathing can reduce stress and enhance recall.

**External prompts** Allow the use of keywords, prompts or flashcards to jog memory.

**Positive affirmation** Reinforce belief in their abilities. A confident mindset can often pave the way for smoother recall.

---

### Teaching tip

Be patient and understanding of the unique recall challenges faced by ADHD students. Offering them varied and multi-sensory revision techniques can be a game-changer. Celebrate their successes, no matter how small, and always focus on progress over perfection. Taking a brain break, or moving on having marked the place they need to come back to, can be really helpful.

# Learning and exams

# IDEA 58

# Independent work planning

When I try to plan my work on my own, it feels like trying to solve a puzzle with too many pieces. I just need a bit of help to see where each piece fits. *Layla, 17*

**Independent work, an essential component of secondary education, demands a level of planning and organisation that can be particularly challenging for students with ADHD. The scatter of tasks, coupled with the ADHD tendency towards impulsivity and distractibility, calls for a structured approach to help these students chart their course effectively.**

### Teaching tip

While guiding ADHD students in planning, it's essential to remember that flexibility is key. Their planning style might differ from the norm, and that's okay. Celebrate their unique approaches while providing structure, and always be open to adapting techniques to suit their individual needs. Your patience and adaptability can pave the way for their planning prowess.

Here are some strategies you can try:

**Start with a brain dump** Encourage students to jot down all tasks without worrying about order. This initial step clears the mind and provides a tangible list to work with.

**Categorise and prioritise** Guide students in grouping tasks by subject or type and then ranking them based on urgency and importance.

**Break tasks into chunks** Help students dissect larger tasks into smaller, manageable steps, making the work feel less overwhelming.

**Allocate time blocks** Introduce the concept of time blocking, where specific chunks of time are dedicated to certain tasks. This provides structure and reduces the chances of distraction.

**Visual planning tools** Recommend tools like mind maps, flowcharts or digital planning apps tailored for ADHD students. Visual representations can aid comprehension and retention.

**IDEA 59**

# Staying on track with assignments

I read the assignment, start with so much enthusiasm, but then realise I've gone off on a tangent. It's like I see a topic, and my brain just wants to explore every related thought, even if it's not in the criteria. *Nathan, 18*

**For students with ADHD, adhering to the criteria of an assignment can be a unique challenge. Their tendency to scan read, potentially missing key details, combined with a natural inclination to explore tangential ideas, often results in deviations from the set path.**

Here are some strategies you can try:

**Highlight key criteria** Encourage students to physically highlight or underline crucial parts of the assignment criteria. This visual cue can serve as a constant reminder.

**Breakdown sessions** Dedicate time to dissect the assignment criteria as a class, discussing each point in detail and clarifying doubts.

**Mind maps and outlines** Guide students in creating mind maps or outlines before starting the assignment. This provides a structured roadmap, helping them stay aligned with the criteria.

**Checkpoints** Set periodic checkpoints where students can review their work against the criteria, ensuring they're on track and making necessary adjustments.

### Teaching tip

Empathy and patience are paramount. Recognise that ADHD students' deviations aren't acts of defiance but rather the nature of their thought processes. Instead of penalising tangents, guide them back to the criteria, appreciating their in-depth explorations while helping them align with the assignment's objectives. Celebrate their creativity and offer structured pathways to channel it effectively.

# IDEA 60

# Revisiting work

A task isn't truly complete until it's been reviewed. Yet, for our ADHD students, this final step of revisiting and checking their work can often feel disproportionately challenging. *Ms. Rowan, Senior Maths Teacher*

**Checking and revising one's work is a crucial component of the learning process. However, for ADHD students, this step can be particularly daunting, largely due to the brain's dopamine levels and the stamina required for sustained attention.**

### Teaching tip

While understanding the neuro-chemical basis of ADHD is essential, it's equally important to approach the challenge with empathy and patience. Tailored strategies, like chunked sessions or reward-based motivation, can be game-changers. However, always be open to adapting your approach based on individual student needs, ensuring they feel supported in every phase of their work. How can you find a solution to a problem together?

Here are some strategies you can try:

**Understand the dopamine link** ADHD is often linked to lower dopamine levels, which play a role in motivation and reward. Revisiting work might not offer the same dopamine 'reward' as new tasks, making it feel more tedious.

**Chunked review sessions** Break the revision process into smaller chunks. Instead of reviewing an entire assignment, focus on sections or particular aspects.

**Use visual aids** Encourage the use of highlighters or coloured pens during the review. This adds a tactile and visual element, making the process more engaging.

**Peer review** Incorporate peer review sessions. Getting feedback from a classmate can be more stimulating and can break the monotony of self-review.

**Reward-based motivation** Introduce a reward system for thorough review sessions. Small incentives can counterbalance the dopamine deficit and motivate ADHD students to revisit their work.

**IDEA 61**

# Editing

*I've poured my thoughts onto the paper, but going back to edit? It feels like trying to find a needle in a haystack. I often miss obvious mistakes or get overwhelmed about where to start. Yasmin, 16*

**Editing and revising written work is a foundational skill in academic progress, demanding keen attention to detail, sound <u>executive function</u> and efficient time management. For ADHD students, these prerequisites can become barriers, making the editing journey arduous.**

Here are some strategies you can try:

**Focused attention exercises** Introduce short exercises to hone attention to detail, like spotting differences in similar texts or proofreading short paragraphs.

**Structured editing approach** Provide a step-by-step guide to editing, breaking down the process from checking content clarity to grammar and punctuation.

**Visual aids and tools** Recommend tools like grammar checkers or software that highlights potential areas for revision. These tools can assist in catching common errors.

**Timed editing sessions** Given the challenges with time and energy management, encourage ADHD students to edit in short, focused bursts, taking breaks in between.

**Collaborative editing** Organise group editing sessions where students can provide feedback on each other's work. Peer insights can spotlight areas the original writer might overlook.

### Teaching tip

Editing requires a blend of skills that ADHD students might find challenging. However, with structured approaches and the right tools, they can navigate this process more confidently. Celebrate their editing efforts, focusing not just on the end product but also on their growth and understanding of the process. Your encouragement can transform their perspective on editing from a challenge to an opportunity.

# IDEA 62

# Exam questions

In the high-stakes world of exams, every word in a question counts. For our ADHD students, ensuring they capture the full essence of each exam question is paramount, lest they lose marks on details they've inadvertently overlooked. *Mrs. Thompson, Exam Coordinator*

**Thoroughly understanding an exam question is pivotal to securing every possible mark. However, ADHD students, with challenges in attention and detail processing, can often bypass nuances or entire segments of a question, inadvertently compromising their grade.**

Here are some strategies you can try:

**Active engagement with questions** Prompt students to underline or highlight key words and criteria in exam questions, ensuring they've acknowledged all facets.

**Exam-specific workshops** Organise sessions that focus on dissecting past exam questions, illuminating common pitfalls and best practices.

**Restate before answering** Cultivate the habit of mentally rephrasing the question before diving into the answer, reinforcing comprehension. A prompt can sometimes be made available as an accommodation, but they can only provide a sounding board and cannot direct a student, other than to say 'look again' if they haven't got it right.

**Visual mapping** For intricate questions, guide students in sketching quick diagrams or flowcharts to break down what's being asked. This can especially aid in multi-part questions.

**Mock exams with peer review** Organise mock exams followed by peer review sessions. This allows students to see different interpretations and understand where they might have veered off track.

> **Teaching tip**
>
> Exams, by their very nature, can be stressful environments. For ADHD students, the combination of time pressure and the need for detail-oriented reading can be particularly daunting. Emphasise the importance of a systematic approach to exam questions, where speed is secondary to comprehension. This mindset shift, coupled with practical strategies, can be the key to unlocking their full exam potential.

# IDEA 63

# Overlooking exam questions

*I've left exams feeling confident, only to discover I missed an entire question. It's not that I didn't know the answer; I just didn't see it.*
*Grace, 15*

**Exams are a culmination of months, even years, of learning. Yet, for ADHD students, the challenge isn't just answering the questions but ensuring they've addressed every single one, a task made challenging by attention fluctuations.**

Here are some strategies you can try:

**Structured exam approach** Teach students a systematic method for tackling exams, such as starting with a full paper scan before diving into answers. If you are encouraging students to go to high mark questions, or ones they are most comfortable with, first, this increases the risk that they will miss questions.

**Use of exam bookmarks** Encourage the use of paper tabs or bookmarks to mark questions they're unsure of or might want to revisit, ensuring they don't unintentionally bypass them.

**Time management reminders** In mock exams, incorporate periodic reminders for students to check they've attempted all questions, helping build this into their exam routine.

**Visual cues** Advise students to draw a quick tick or cross against each question number as they go along, providing a visual confirmation of addressed questions.

**Post-exam check** Cultivate the habit of a final review, where students go back to ensure every question has an answer before time is up.

### Teaching tip

While content revision is essential, it's equally crucial to train ADHD students in exam strategies that counteract inattentiveness. Simple practices, like a post-exam check or using visual cues, can make a world of difference. The goal is to provide them with the tools to present their knowledge comprehensively.

### Taking it further

Accommodations such as extra time, prompts, or movement breaks can be instrumental for ADHD students. These adjustments are about ensuring all students have an equitable opportunity to showcase their knowledge and skills. It's crucial for schools to have students with ADHD assessed by the Exams Access Arrangement Assessor, as they pinpoint specific needs and recommend tailored accommodations.

# IDEA 64

# Understanding intricate questions

*Complex questions are like intricate puzzles; each word plays a pivotal role in deciphering the bigger picture. For our ADHD students, these puzzles can sometimes seem more convoluted, demanding a deeper level of guidance to unlock their meaning.*
*Ms. Green, Geography Teacher*

**In secondary education, the ability to comprehend and respond to complex questions becomes increasingly crucial. ADHD students, who face challenges in sustained attention and detail processing, can find these questions particularly daunting, necessitating tailored strategies to aid their understanding.**

### Teaching tip

Complex questions may pose an amplified challenge for ADHD students. Arm them with tools and strategies that demystify these questions. Through consistent practice, feedback and collaborative learning, you can empower these students to navigate complexity with confidence and precision.

### Taking it further

Poorly worded questions can be an added tax on an already challenged **executive function**. It can help to allow the student to reword the question before they go on to answer it. If you can do this in lessons, they should be able to bypass this step eventually, which can pay dividends in actual exams.

Here are some strategies you can try:

**Active reading techniques** Encourage students to read questions aloud, annotate as they go, or paraphrase in their own words to ensure comprehension.

**Dissect and discuss** Dedicate class time to breaking down intricate questions, illuminating each component and its significance.

**Visual aids** Use flowcharts, diagrams or mind maps to represent complex questions visually, aiding in clarity and understanding.

**Practice with feedback** Regularly expose students to complex questions in practice sessions, followed by discussions on their interpretations and any misconceptions.

**Peer explainers** Organise sessions where students take turns explaining their understanding of a complex question to peers. This reciprocal teaching can clarify doubts and solidify comprehension.

**IDEA 65**

# Handwriting challenges

*I've got so many ideas racing in my head, but getting them down on paper neatly? It's like trying to catch lightning in a bottle.*
*Mateo, 14*

**While handwriting might seem like a basic skill, for many ADHD students it represents a convergence of cognitive, motor and attentional challenges. Their handwriting can be inconsistent, hurried or even illegible, not due to carelessness but because of the underlying intricacies of their neurodiversity.**

For some students, handwriting is always going to be a challenge in that it might not conform to what is expected, and may or may not be legible. Here are some strategies you can try:

**Fine motor skill activities** Introduce exercises that enhance fine motor skills, like clay modelling, LEGO® construction, bead threading, ball squeezing, scissor work and targeted drawing tasks.

**Specialised writing tools** Provide thicker or ergonomic pens or pencils designed to aid grip and control, making the act of writing more comfortable.

**Alternative writing methods** Explore the use of lined or raised paper, or writing slopes, which can assist in maintaining consistent handwriting.

**Regular handwriting practice** Dedicate short, focused sessions to handwriting exercises, gradually building stamina and consistency.

**Technology integration** For students with severe handwriting difficulties, consider introducing typing or voice-to-text software as an alternative means of capturing their ideas.

### Teaching tip

Approaching handwriting challenges with patience and understanding is key. Recognise that for ADHD students, the act of writing encompasses more than just penmanship – it's about translating their rapid, multifaceted thoughts into linear, coherent script. Celebrate their progress, provide tools to aid their journey, and always prioritise capturing their knowledge over the perfection of their script.

## IDEA 66

# High-stakes handwriting

When I'm under pressure, it's like there's a traffic jam in my brain. I'm trying to think creatively, remember the criteria and write legibly all at once. It's overwhelming. *Isla, 14*

High-pressure writing scenarios, such as exams or timed essays, amplify the challenges ADHD students face with handwriting. Balancing the <u>executive function</u> demands of organising thoughts, adhering to criteria and producing creative content, all while maintaining legible handwriting, can be a Herculean task.

Here are some strategies you can try:

**Pre-writing brain dumps** Before diving into the task, allow students a few minutes to jot down their initial thoughts. This clears the cognitive space and provides a roadmap.

**Structured writing frameworks** Provide students with templates or frameworks to organise their thoughts and adhere to criteria under pressure.

**Handwriting drills** Incorporate regular sessions focused on improving writing speed and legibility, ensuring students are better prepared for timed tasks.

**Mindfulness and breathing exercises** To calm nerves and enhance focus before high-pressure writing tasks, try deep breathing.

**Practice in real-time scenarios** Organise mock tests or timed writing.

**Shift your expectations** If it is legible, that's good enough. Take the stress out and the handwriting will be just that little bit better.

**Use tech** Students can do their work on laptops or tablets. Yes, even in exam situations, but this needs to be pre-approved with the SENCO and Exams Officer through an Exams Access Arrangement Assessment.

### Taking it further

In a rapidly evolving world, the rigid standards of 'conforming' handwriting seem increasingly outmoded. In our digital age, many adults predominantly type or text, with handwriting restricted to brief notes or signatures. Emphasising legibility over conformity better equips students for real-world scenarios. Rather than penalising students for not adhering to a specific handwriting mould, it's more pragmatic and constructive to ensure they can convey their ideas clearly and legibly, just as they would in most professional and personal settings.

**IDEA 67**

# Spelling, punctuation and grammar

I know the rules when I read them, but when I'm writing, it's like they vanish. Trying to remember spellings, where the comma goes, and getting my tenses right — it's a juggling act. *Leo, 14*

**Spelling, punctuation, and grammar (SPaG) are fundamental components of effective written communication. However, for ADHD students, consistently applying these rules can be a formidable challenge due to the intricacies of <u>executive function</u> and the demands on working memory.**

Here are some strategies you can try:

**Chunked learning** Break SPaG rules into manageable chunks, focusing on mastering one aspect before moving to the next.

**Interactive activities** Use games, quizzes or apps that reinforce SPaG concepts in engaging ways, aiding retention.

**Visual aids** Introduce mnemonic devices, charts or diagrams to represent grammar rules or tricky spellings, providing visual cues to support working memory.

**Consistent practice** Dedicate short, regular sessions to SPaG exercises, ensuring repetition and reinforcement.

**Peer review** Incorporate peer editing in class assignments, allowing students to spot and correct SPaG errors collaboratively.

### Teaching tip

Recognising the nuanced challenges ADHD students face with SPaG is essential. It's not merely about understanding the rules but juggling them in real-time with content creation. Offering targeted support, regular practice and a dose of patience can go a long way in helping them navigate the SPaG maze with increasing confidence.

### Bonus idea ★

Timed writing tasks bring an inherent pressure, demanding content accuracy and precise SPaG rules. Get students to practise SPaG exercises under timed conditions, or mock exams with an emphasis on SPaG. Post-test reviews can pinpoint areas of improvement.

# IDEA 68

# Streamlined content presentation

*When I write, it's like a floodgate of ideas. I want to include everything because it all feels important.* Raj, 17

**Presenting content in a concise, clear manner is an essential skill, especially in academic settings. For ADHD students, their processing challenges can make discerning between crucial and supplementary information difficult, often leading to an overload of content in their presentations or writings.**

Here are some strategies you can try:

**Prioritisation workshops** Conduct sessions that focus on distinguishing between main and supplementary information, teaching students how to prioritise where they focus their time and energy.

**Mind mapping** Encourage the use of mind maps or flowcharts to visually represent ideas, helping students see the hierarchy of information.

**Leaning in to the criteria** Make sure the task criteria are clearly stated for all lessons, even those where the criteria is loose.

**Structured writing templates** Provide frameworks that guide students in organising their content, ensuring a balance between depth and breadth.

**Peer review sessions** Allow students to review each other's work, offering feedback on areas that might be redundant or overly detailed.

**Reflection and refinement** After a writing task, guide students in reflecting on their content choices, discussing what was essential and what could have been left out.

> **Taking it further**
>
> Try using sticky notes or index cards with the criteria for tasks listed. This isn't just about completing an assignment. It's about mastering the crucial life skill of writing to criteria.

# IDEA 69

# Expanding content

Sometimes, my mind feels blank. I read the criteria and want to meet it, but I just can't find any words or ideas. *Layla, 16*

**Crafting content that meets set criteria is a foundational aspect of academic assignments. However, for some ADHD students, the challenge lies not in condensing a plethora of ideas, but in generating enough to adequately address the given criteria.**

Here are some strategies you can try:

**Brain-dumping sessions** Dedicate time to group brain-dumping, allowing students to feed off each other's ideas and expand their own.

**Mind mapping** Encourage the use of visual tools like mind maps to help students explore and branch out from a central idea, fleshing out content.

**Research and exploration** Guide students in researching topics, providing them with resources and materials to spark thoughts and ideas.

**Questioning techniques** Use open-ended questions to prompt deeper thinking and exploration of a topic, helping students delve into various facets.

**Share examples** Examples from within the class, or provided by the teacher, allow students to see the bigger picture and possible ways to progress.

**Make it relevant** Is there a way to embed the task in something that is interesting to this student? Whether it's a football team, a pop star, a TV series or whatever is meaningful to the student.

### Teaching tip

If students struggle to generate content, approach the challenge with patience and a toolkit of strategies. Remember that for ADHD students, this struggle isn't indicative of a lack of understanding but often a momentary lapse in idea generation. By fostering a collaborative and explorative environment, you can help them bridge the content gap and meet the set criteria with confidence.

### Taking it further

ADHDers possess an 'interest-based nervous system', which means their engagement, focus and productivity are heightened when working on something that genuinely interests them. Tailoring tasks to the student can transform potential struggles into moments of deep learning and insight.

# IDEA 70

# Word-based maths

Word-based maths problems are like mini-stories with hidden numerical clues. For our ADHD students, extracting these clues from the narrative can feel like a multi-layered maze, especially when their **executive functions** are pulled in different directions. *Mr. Carter, Advanced Maths Instructor*

**Maths problems presented as stories or scenarios, such as calculating change from a shopping trip, add an additional layer of comprehension to the mathematical task. For ADHD students, this blend of literacy and numeracy can present a unique challenge, as it demands simultaneous engagement of different executive functions.**

### Teaching tip

Delving into word-based maths problems requires a delicate balance of language comprehension and mathematical reasoning. For ADHD students, this balance can be challenging, given the multiple executive functions at play. A methodical, step-by-step approach, combined with consistent practice, can help demystify these textual conundrums, allowing students to tackle them with increased confidence.

Here are some strategies you can try:

**Highlight key information** Teach students to underline or highlight crucial numerical details in the question, like prices or quantities.

**Break it down** Encourage them to rewrite the problem step-by-step, simplifying the narrative and focusing only on the mathematical operations required.

**Use visual aids** Suggest drawing a simple picture or diagram, such as items bought and their prices, to visually represent the problem.

**Repetition and familiarity** Provide various similar problems for practice, allowing students to recognise patterns and become familiar with the structure of word-based maths problems.

**Peer collaboration** Let students work in pairs or small groups to discuss and solve problems together, allowing them to share strategies and insights.

**IDEA 71**

# Mental arithmetic

*When I try to do maths in my head, numbers start to jumble, and I lose track. I've found that jotting things down helps, even if it's just a few key numbers. Dylan, 15*

**The art of mental arithmetic is a core skill in numeracy, demanding quick thinking and robust working memory. However, for ADHD students, the inherent challenges of their neurodiversity can make calculating in their head feel like navigating a constantly shifting maze.**

Here are some strategies you can try:

**Reinforce basics** Ensure that foundational arithmetic skills, like basic addition or multiplication tables, are solidified, as they often form the building blocks of mental calculations.

**Encourage note-taking** Teach students that it's okay to jot down key figures or steps, especially when the mental load becomes too overwhelming.

**Chunking techniques** Introduce strategies to break down larger problems into smaller, more manageable chunks, making mental calculations easier.

**Memory aids** Use mnemonic devices, rhymes or patterns to help students remember common calculations or mathematical relationships.

**Practice with feedback** Engage students in regular mental arithmetic drills, followed by discussions to share strategies, mistakes and insights.

### Teaching tip

Embracing the unique challenges ADHD students face with mental arithmetic means understanding their working memory dynamics. It's essential to foster an environment where they feel no shame in writing down intermediary steps or using tools to aid their calculations. By offering tailored strategies and continuous support, you can help them bolster their mental arithmetic skills, building both competence and confidence.

# IDEA 72

# Instinctive answers

Some of our ADHD students possess a remarkable knack for intuitively grasping the solution, but then find themselves at a loss when asked to retrace their thought process. It's like they've sprinted to the finish line but can't map out the route they took. *Mrs. Fletcher, Advanced Maths Instructor*

**The ability to swiftly and instinctively arrive at an answer is impressive, but in academic settings, the journey — the 'working' — is often as important as the destination. For ADHD students, this dichotomy can be challenging, as their brain might leap to conclusions, leaving them unable to articulate the steps they took mentally.**

Here are some strategies you can try:

**Slow down and reflect** Encourage students to pause after they find an answer, taking a moment to mentally retrace their steps before writing anything down.

**Practise verbal articulation** Have students explain their thought process out loud, even if it's just to themselves, to reinforce their understanding.

**Use visual aids** Suggest drawing diagrams, flowcharts or even simple doodles to help map out their thought process visually.

**Structured problem solving** Introduce methodologies or templates for solving specific types of problems, guiding students in a step-by-step manner.

**Peer collaboration** Let students work with peers to solve problems collaboratively, allowing them to discuss and articulate their thought processes together.

### Teaching tip

Recognise and celebrate the intuitive problem-solving abilities of ADHD students, but also emphasise the importance of 'showing their work'. This not only solidifies their understanding but is crucial for academic assessments. By providing tools and practices to help them articulate their thought processes, you empower them to shine both intuitively and methodically.

# IDEA 73

# Transcribing information accurately

I start copying a sentence, then when I look back up, I've lost my place. It's like trying to follow a moving target with everything else around it being a distraction. *Imogen, 11*

**Transferring information from the board to one's notebook is a common classroom task. Yet, for ADHD students, this seemingly straightforward activity can become complex, influenced by challenges such as eye tracking, attention maintenance and working memory.**

Here are some strategies you can try:

**Colour coding** Use different colours on the board for different points or sections, providing a visual cue to help students track their position.

**Chunking information** Break the information on the board into smaller, more digestible sections, allowing students to copy in stages without feeling overwhelmed.

**Verbal reinforcement** As you write on the board, vocalise the content, helping to reinforce what students are copying through auditory means.

**Use of technology** Consider sharing board content digitally, allowing students to access it on devices or in print, reducing the need for manual copying.

**Peer assistance** Encourage collaborative note-taking, where students can cross-check and fill in gaps in each other's notes.

### Teaching tip

Understanding the multifaceted challenges ADHD students face when copying from the board is the first step in providing effective support. Their struggles often stem from a combination of eye-tracking difficulties, fleeting attention and limited working memory. By implementing supportive strategies and offering alternative methods for content absorption, you can ensure that these students capture essential information accurately and efficiently.

## IDEA 74

# Repeated reading distractions

For many of our students, reading is a serene river flow; for our ADHD students, it's often navigating rapids. Their path is punctuated by distractions, diverging thoughts, and the frequent need to circle back and re-read. *Mrs. Thompson, Head of English*

**While reading is a foundational academic skill, for ADHD students it can be akin to an obstacle course. Their journey through a text is often disrupted by an array of internal and external distractions, leading to frequent pauses and reflections, and the recurrent need to re-read.**

### Teaching tip

Empathy is crucial when supporting ADHD students in their reading journey. Understand that for them, reading isn't just a linear path; it's filled with hurdles. By acknowledging the inherent difficulty and equipping them with strategies to manage and overcome these challenges, you can help transform reading from a daunting task to a more navigable adventure.

Here are some strategies you can try:

**Active engagement** Encourage the use of tools like highlighters or sticky notes, prompting students to interact with the text actively, anchoring their attention.

**Structured reading breaks** Recommend deliberate, short breaks at regular intervals, which allows students a moment to regroup and refocus.

**Guided reading tools** Suggest tools such as reading rulers or finger tracing, assisting students in maintaining their line of sight and progression.

**Distraction-minimised environment** Designate or suggest quiet, clutter-free zones for reading, minimising potential external distractions.

**Grounding techniques** Introduce refocusing exercises to centre students' attention, equipping them to redirect when their thoughts drift. Teach narratives such as 'It is okay that I got distracted. I'm back now. What was I doing?' There should be no judgement placed on losing focus as that depletes energy and blocks the way back to task.

**IDEA 75**

# Inattentive scan reading

I often find myself just scanning through a page, thinking I've got it. But when I discuss it or get quizzed, I realise I've missed major points. It's like watching a film and missing the main scenes. *Raj, 16*

**Scan reading can be an efficient way to get a general idea of a text, but for ADHD students, this often unintentional skimming can lead to significant gaps in understanding. The underlying inattentiveness means they might bypass critical information or context, impacting comprehension.**

Here are some strategies you can try:

**Purposeful reading** Encourage students to set specific goals before reading, such as identifying the main idea or noting down key events, to guide their focus.

**Annotation techniques** Teach students to underline, highlight or jot notes in the margins, promoting active engagement with the text.

**Chunking text** Break the content into smaller sections or paragraphs, prompting students to pause, reflect and ensure they've grasped each segment before moving on.

**Discussion and recap** After reading, engage students in discussions or quick summaries, reinforcing comprehension and identifying any missed details.

**Guided reading sessions** Organise sessions where texts are read aloud and discussed in real-time, ensuring students are aligned with the content's core messages.

> **Teaching tip**
>
> Recognising the tendency of ADHD students to inadvertently skim-read is pivotal. Their inattentiveness isn't a reflection of their intelligence or willingness to learn but rather a facet of their neurodiversity. By providing tools and strategies to anchor their attention and deepen their engagement, you can help ensure they extract the richness and nuance from every text they encounter.

## IDEA 76

# Misreading tendencies

*When I read, I'm always on the lookout for the exciting parts, the bits that spark my interest. But sometimes, I realise I've skimmed over essential details or misread words because they didn't immediately grab me.* Finn, 14

**For ADHD students, reading isn't just about absorbing information; it's an intricate dance of dopamine-driven interest and the challenges of maintaining focus. This dynamic can lead to misreading, particularly through scan reading, <u>confirmation bias</u>, or losing their place in the text.**

### Teaching tip
Understanding the unique reading challenges of ADHD students requires empathy and patience. It's not that they aren't keen to grasp the material, but their neurodiversity often directs their focus towards what's immediately stimulating. By introducing strategies that harness their strengths and mitigate their challenges, you can guide them towards a more balanced and comprehensive reading experience.

Here are some strategies you can try:

**Active engagement** Encourage students to underline, circle or annotate as they read, ensuring even the 'less exciting' parts of the text get attention.

**Reading aloud** Suggest reading portions of text aloud, aiding in comprehension and reducing the chances of misreading prefixes or suffixes.

**Guided focus** Break down reading assignments into sections, setting specific questions or goals for each, to ensure comprehensive coverage of the material.

**Acknowledging bias** Discuss the concept of confirmation bias, teaching students to be aware of their tendencies to seek out only dopamine-driven, relevant information.

**Use of tools** Offer tools like reading rulers or digital highlighters to help students maintain their place, ensuring they don't inadvertently skip or misread sections.

**IDEA 77**

# Speed of thought vs. hand

My thoughts come rushing in, and I'm trying to get them all down on paper. Later, I realise I've written the same word twice or missed one out completely, even if it sounded perfect in my head. *Zoe, 16*

**Writing for ADHD students can sometimes be a frantic race to capture a whirlwind of thoughts. This urgency, combined with potential co-occurring challenges like dyslexia, can lead to repeated or omitted words and letters, often overlooked even upon review.**

Here are some strategies you can try:

**Pace and pause** Encourage students to periodically pause as they write, giving their hands a moment to catch up to their rapid thoughts.

**Multi-sensory approaches** Incorporate tools that allow for auditory or tactile feedback, such as speech-to-text software, to help in capturing their ideas more accurately.

**Recognising co-occurrence** Educate students about the potential overlap of ADHD and dyslexia, fostering an awareness that can aid in understanding and addressing their writing challenges. See the Bloomsbury Education  website for information about teaching this.

**Structured review** Introduce a systematic approach to revising their work, focusing on common errors like repetition or omission.

**Peer review** Encourage collaborative writing exercises where students can review and correct each other's work, providing fresh eyes to spot unnoticed errors.

> **Teaching tip**
>
> Understanding the intricacies of ADHD students' writing challenges is essential. Their errors often stem from the sheer speed of their cognition rather than a lack of effort. By equipping them with strategies that acknowledge and address the root of these challenges, you can support them in articulating their vibrant thoughts with clarity and precision.

# IDEA 78

# Tech to aid writing nuances

*Getting my thoughts down can be a sprint, and sometimes words get doubled up or forgotten. But when I started using tech tools, it felt like I had an extra set of eyes and hands helping me out.* Zoe, 16

**For ADHD students, the act of writing can be akin to chasing a speeding train of thoughts. Coupled with potential co-existing conditions like dyslexia, this can result in chaotic or unclear writing, but with the aid of technology these challenges can be addressed and even transformed into strengths.**

Here are some strategies you can try:

**Speech-to-text software** Encourage the use of dictation tools that can transcribe their spoken words, allowing their hands to keep pace with their thoughts.

**Automated writing assistants** Introduce software like Grammarly® or Microsoft Editor® that can highlight and correct repeated words, omissions and other common errors in real-time.

**Awareness of co-occurrence** Foster an understanding of the potential overlap between ADHD and dyslexia, and explore tech tools specifically designed for dyslexic support.

**Digital reviews** Teach students to use features like 'track changes' in word processors, facilitating a systematic approach to revising their work.

**Collaborative platforms** Use platforms like Google Docs™, where students can collaboratively write and review in real-time, benefiting from peer insights and corrections.

### Teaching tip

Embrace the digital age's offerings to support the unique writing challenges of ADHD students. Their potential writing missteps are not indicative of their effort or intelligence but reflect the speed of their cognition. By integrating technology into their writing process, you not only provide a safety net for common errors but empower them to harness their rapid thoughts effectively.

# Impulsivity, attribution and justice

Part 8

# IDEA 79

# Promoting impulse control

*My thoughts race, and my actions follow. I've done something before I have even thought about it.* Mia, 15

**Impulse control can be a significant challenge for learners with ADHD, often leading to disruptions in the classroom and wider school. The right strategies and understanding can guide these learners towards better self-regulation and fewer impulsive acts.**

### Taking it further

Collaborate with parents and caregivers. Share strategies and insights to ensure that impulse control techniques are consistent both at school and home. This cohesive approach can be beneficial for the student's overall development.

Here are some strategies you can try:

**Understand the underlying causes** Impulsivity in ADHD learners isn't about defiance; it's often a result of their brain's wiring. Being empathetic can make a big difference.

**Create a predictable environment** Structure and routine can help ADHD students anticipate what's next, reducing impulsive outbursts. Establish a consistent daily schedule and communicate when there may be a change.

**Positive reinforcement** Instead of focusing on negative behaviours, reward positive ones. Praise students when they exhibit patience or thoughtful decision-making.

**Offer breaks** Allow short breaks to move around or engage in physical activity. This can help dissipate pent-up energy and also reduce impulsivity.

**Teach delayed gratification** Encourage students to count to ten before they respond. Gradually they should be able to do this more independently. Remember that we are striving for better, not perfect, as 'perfect' is an unattainable standard.

**Open communication** Encourage students to express their feelings and frustrations before they boil over. Sometimes, just talking can help them understand and manage their impulses better. Remember that all emotions are valid, even if the behaviours that follow need to be addressed.

**IDEA 80**

# Effective recovery after an impulsive act

I needed a chance to start over, but everyone just stayed mad at me, so I figured there was no point trying. *Charlie, 16*

**In the hustle and bustle of a school setting, impulsive acts can sometimes disrupt the learning environment. However, the focus shouldn't be just on the act itself, but on the steps taken afterwards to understand, make amends and prevent future occurrences.**

Here are some strategies you can try:

**Acknowledge and reflect** Reflection and restorative communication can help students understand the reasons behind their actions so that they can gain some control over this trait.

**Open dialogue** Facilitate a conversation between the involved parties to resolve conflicts and to help to foster understanding and empathy.

**Apologise and make amends** Teach students the importance of a sincere apology. Consider ways they might make amends through positive deeds.

**Seek guidance** Use the school's pastoral care or counselling services.

**Implement preventative measures** Introduce techniques such as counting to ten before reacting, or seeking a trusted individual to talk things over before making decisions.

**Educate the peer group** Organise classroom sessions on impulse control, understanding ADHD and promoting empathy. When peers understand, they're more likely to be supportive and less judgemental.

**Consistent monitoring** Keep an eye on triggers or patterns that lead to impulsive acts. Understanding these can help in devising strategies to prevent them.

### Teaching tip

'What were you thinking?' might seem like an obvious question, but the answer might be that they weren't. They might be thinking 'I wonder what might happen if...' but their inhibition control was offline and they were acting on impulse. ADHDers can inhibit their impulses, but it is like a willpower tank that runs low over time. We can increase willpower capacity through praise and recognition and opportunities to talk. We diminish willpower tank capacity when we use shame and place students in stressful situations.

# IDEA 81

# Difficulty learning from mistakes

Navigating the process of learning from mistakes involves patience, empathy and a supportive approach that encourages growth.
*Mr. Jackson, Headteacher*

**Learning from mistakes can be intricate, especially for students with ADHD, who may grapple with the underlying reasons behind their errors. By employing empathetic strategies and reinforcing positive growth, educators can help these students transform setbacks into opportunities for improvement.**

Here are some strategies you can try:

**Empathetic understanding** Approach mistakes with understanding rather than frustration. Acknowledge that factors beyond carelessness can contribute to repeated errors, and provide a safe space to express challenges.

**Timely feedback** Offer feedback promptly after a mistake occurs. When students connect the feedback to the action, it enhances comprehension of the error and its implications.

**Encourage self-reflection** Guide students to reflect on their actions and decisions. Use open-ended questions to prompt self-realisation, enabling them to identify the factors that led to the mistake.

**Patience after emotional episodes** After any intense emotional episodes like meltdowns or shutdowns, allow students time to recover fully before engaging in further discussion.

**Practice for reinforcement** Once the mistake is understood, encourage practice of the correct action. Repetition reinforces the learning process and helps prevent future errors.

**Celebrate improvement** Recognise even small steps towards improvement. Celebrating progress boosts students' confidence and motivation to continue growing.

---

**Bonus idea** ★

Create a learning journal, where students can document their mistakes, the actions they took and the outcomes. Encourage them to reflect on what they learned from each experience.

## IDEA 82

# Lying to avoid conflict

*I panicked and said it wasn't me, even though I knew it was obviously me. Then I was stuck and in even more trouble.* Mohammed, 15

**Lying in young people usually isn't born out of malice, but rather as a defence mechanism to avoid conflict or potential repercussions. Understanding the reasons behind such behaviours is crucial for educators and parents alike, to guide students towards more authentic and open communication.**

Here are some strategies you can try:

**Identify the underlying fear** Try to understand what the student feared might happen if they told the truth. Was it fear of punishment, causing disappointment, or triggering an argument?

**Consider impulsivity** Did they lie on impulse? If so, it can be helpful to point this possibility out and give them a chance to reset the conversation and start on a level and open footing.

**Promote a safe environment** Foster a classroom atmosphere where students feel safe expressing themselves without fear of harsh judgement or punishment.

**Open channels of communication** Encourage students to share their feelings and concerns. Let them know that their voices are valued.

**Teach conflict resolution** Equip students with tools and strategies to handle disagreements and confrontations in a healthy, constructive manner.

**Discuss the value of honesty** Use stories or real-life examples to highlight the long-term benefits of honesty over the temporary relief of lying.

**Reinforce trust** When students are honest, especially in challenging situations, commend them for their bravery and reinforce that trust.

**Seek counselling** Persistent lying might indicate deeper emotional or psychological issues. School counsellors can provide insights and support.

### Teaching tip

There is a lot to be said for being a psychologically safe adult for young people. Addressing the act of lying requires sensitivity and patience. By approaching the situation with understanding and a genuine desire to help, educators can guide students away from falsehoods borne from fear, and towards open, honest communication.

### Taking it further

Collaborate with parents and guardians. They can reinforce the learning at home, further helping students internalise the lessons from their mistakes. This should always be constructive, and sanctions in school shouldn't be continued at home, or vice versa.

## IDEA 83

# Owning up to mistakes

*Every mistake I make feels like a giant spotlight on me. I know I need to own it, but sometimes it's just too hard.* Mia, 16

**For individuals with ADHD, acknowledging errors can often come with an amplified sense of shame or guilt. Teaching the art of healthy attribution can transform these moments into opportunities for growth and resilience.**

### Taking it further

Research shows that ADHDers can often have **unhealthy attribution**. This shows up in phrases like 'It's not my fault. They started it'. In this case, the young person isn't understanding their role in what happened and is attributing blame or responsibility externally, or away from themselves. It is a good idea to acknowledge the actions of the other party, but to then bring it back to the young person before you. They might resist this notion at first, but with repeated messages this tends to be understood, and incidences reduce.

Here are some strategies you can try:

**Promote a growth mindset** Emphasise that mistakes are a natural part of the learning process. It's not the error that defines us, but how we respond to it.

**Distinguish between blame and responsibility** Teach that while they may not be to blame for every situation, taking responsibility for their actions empowers them to make positive changes.

**Provide constructive feedback** Instead of focusing solely on what went wrong, offer guidance on how to make it right.

**Model accountability** Demonstrate through actions that everyone makes mistakes and that owning up to them is a sign of strength.

**Encourage self-reflection** Provide tools and strategies to help students reflect on situations, understand their reactions, and plan for better outcomes in the future.

**Use storytelling** Incorporate storytelling and narratives of famous personalities who overcame challenges, made mistakes, and used them as stepping stones to success. This provides relatable context and illustrates that everyone, regardless of their background or challenges, can learn and grow from their experiences.

# IDEA 84

# Embracing restorative justice

In the journey of understanding ADHD, **restorative justice** shines a light on connection, empathy, and true resolution. *Mr. Brown, Pastoral Lead*

**Traditional disciplinary measures can often misinterpret the unique challenges faced by students with ADHD, leading to feelings of isolation and misunderstanding. Restorative justice, with its emphasis on dialogue and reconciliation, offers a more inclusive approach that respects the ADHD experience and fosters genuine growth.**

Here are some strategies you can try:

**Focus on relationships** Recognise that behaviours of ADHD students often stem from their neurodiverse challenges, not defiance. Prioritise understanding and rebuilding connections over punitive actions.

**Engage in ADHD-informed dialogue** Facilitate discussions where students, especially those with ADHD, can express their feelings and perspectives. This can lead to mutual understanding and empathy.

**Accountability with compassion** Encourage students with ADHD to understand the impact of their actions, but also ensure that the school community understands the unique challenges of ADHD.

**Collaborative problem solving** Involve ADHD students in the process of devising solutions. This not only addresses the immediate issue but also instils a sense of agency and inclusion.

**Continuous reflection with ADHD in mind** Regularly reassess your restorative practices, ensuring they cater to the unique needs of ADHD students and promote a conducive learning environment.

### Teaching tip

Incorporating restorative justice with a focus on ADHD can revolutionise the classroom environment, making it more inclusive and understanding. It offers students with ADHD an opportunity to be understood, valued and supported in their academic journey.

### Taking it further

Some key principles of restorative practice that you can use in the classroom are building relationships between students, teachers and staff, involving everyone, focusing on the future, and empowering students.

# IDEA 85

# A heightened sense of justice

Understanding and nurturing the strong sense of justice in students with ADHD can empower them to become advocates for fairness and positive change. *Ms. Carter, Politics Teacher*

**Individuals with ADHD often possess an intense and profound sense of justice, leading them to passionately stand up against perceived inequities. This characteristic, though challenging at times, can also be a driving force for positive change and advocacy.**

### Teaching tip

It is really important to help students understand that they cannot take responsibility for others. Not by way of taking on someone else's situation as their own, nor by trying to correct who or what is responsible for the situation. They can be part of the solution by being an ally to someone in need, but the only person they can actually take responsibility for is themselves.

Here are some strategies you can try:

**Recognise the passion** Acknowledge that strong reactions to injustice are rooted in genuine passion for fairness and equality.

**Open discussions** Create a safe space for students to openly discuss their views on justice and fairness, encouraging them to share their thoughts.

**Promote nuanced thinking** Guide students in understanding that justice can sometimes be complex, and situations might not have clear right or wrong answers.

**Empower advocacy** Encourage them to channel their passion for justice into constructive advocacy efforts, such as participating in school clubs or community projects.

**Provide role models** Introduce them to historical figures or contemporary role models who have effectively used their sense of justice to bring about positive change.

**Offer guidance** Be a source of support by providing guidance on effective ways to communicate their concerns and advocate for change.

# IDEA 86

# Advocacy and over-involvement

When I see someone struggling, I feel it deep inside. It's like I can't help but jump in, even if I don't have the whole picture. *Eli, 16*

**ADHD individuals often possess a compelling drive to advocate for others, drawn from deep wells of empathy and a strong sense of justice. However, this passion can sometimes steer them into becoming overly involved, blurring the lines between supporting and overshadowing.**

Here are some strategies you can try:

**Awareness building** Encourage students to recognise and understand their inherent drive to assist and where it might lead them astray.

**Pause and reflect** Teach the value of taking a moment to assess a situation before diving in, ensuring they have all the relevant information.

**Define boundaries** Emphasise the importance of knowing when to step in and when to step back, allowing the individual or cause at the centre to remain the focal point.

**Channel the energy** Guide students towards structured avenues, such as school clubs or community initiatives, where they can positively express their advocacy.

**Feedback is gold** Encourage students to seek feedback from peers and those that they're trying to help, ensuring their actions are genuinely beneficial.

### Teaching tip

In class discussions or group activities, simulate scenarios where advocacy is needed, allowing students to practise their response in a controlled environment. This will provide them with practical experience and an opportunity to reflect on their approach.

**IDEA 87**

# Uber empathy

Students with ADHD often demonstrate profound empathy. While this can lead to genuine connections, it also means they might find themselves inadvertently drawn into others' battles. *Mrs. Davies, Head of Pastoral Care*

---

**Uber empathy, frequently observed in students with ADHD, encompasses their heightened capacity to intensely connect with and understand the emotions of others. Emotional reactions about something that happened to somebody else might not make sense to us, but that doesn't mean the ADHD child isn't feeling it.**

---

### Teaching tip

Understanding the depth of ADHD students' emotional connections can transform our approach in the classroom. By recognising, guiding and supporting these students, we can harness their unique perspective while also teaching them ways to protect their emotional wellbeing.

Here are some strategies you can try:

**Acknowledge the depth** Recognise that ADHD students can experience other people's emotions as deeply as if they were their own.

**Highlight the positive** Emphasise the positive aspects of uber empathy, such as forming deep connections and offer genuine support.

**Equip with emotional tools** Mindfulness and reflection exercises can help students manage their intense emotions and discern when to step back.

**Encourage open dialogue** Create an environment where students can discuss their feelings and experiences related to their heightened empathy without judgement.

**Educate classmates** Inform peers about the concept of uber empathy in ADHD, cultivating an understanding and supportive classroom.

**Consult specialist support** Consider enlisting the help of school counsellors or therapists to guide students in balancing their deep empathy without overextending themselves.

**Guide in navigating conflicts** Students with intense emotional involvement might find conflicts challenging. Offer support in resolving disagreements with empathy and perspective.

# Homework, attendance and independent development

Part 9

# IDEA 88

# Asking for and accepting help

I'm not going to ask for help. Partly because I don't trust teachers to actually help, and partly because I don't want to stand out.
*Damion, 15*

**For students with ADHD, reaching out for guidance can be overshadowed by feelings of vulnerability or fear of being perceived differently. As educators, it's imperative to cultivate a classroom environment where seeking assistance is seen as a stepping stone to success, not a sign of weakness.**

Here are some strategies you can try:

**Be a safe adult** At the very least, make sure your learners don't feel judged or shamed by your words and actions. Stay open and warm, and they are more likely to ask for and accept help.

**Pre-agreed communication** There are subtle ways a learner can communicate a need for support that can be pre-agreed. For example, placing their ruler on the top edge of the table.

**Cultivate a safe environment** Foster a classroom atmosphere where mistakes are seen as learning opportunities, not failures. Highlight stories of famous personalities who thrived with the help of others.

**Model the behaviour you want to see** Make errors, accidentally on purpose, so that learners can see you recover from them. They won't lose respect for you – you will reposition yourself as an attainable role-model.

**Empower through choice** When offering assistance, give options on how they'd like to receive it. This promotes autonomy and respects their individual learning styles.

**Acknowledge efforts** Recognise and applaud when students take the initiative to ask for help. This positive reinforcement can motivate them and others to seek assistance in the future.

### Teaching tip

There is so much to be said for creating a safe collaborative space where different strengths are accepted and struggles supported. This is hard to achieve in secondary schools currently, but I encourage you to talk positively about neurodiversity and positive role models, as well as allowing learners to see you as attainable and fallible, yet competent.

# IDEA 89

# Forgetfulness

For some, a forgotten pencil or PE kit isn't a sign of carelessness, but a manifestation of deeper challenges. *Mrs. Davies, Year 8 Form Tutor*

**It's a common scene: students arriving without their kit or essential equipment, prompting assumptions about their commitment or attention. However, particularly for those with neurodiverse challenges like ADHD, this forgetfulness is often rooted in deeper cognitive and emotional struggles.**

Here are some strategies you can try:

**Acknowledge executive function challenges** Recognise that neurodiverse students might struggle with organisation due to challenges with executive function.

**Spot signs of overwhelm** Understand that for some, the pressures of school can overshadow task reminders. Overwhelm often manifests as being flustered, irritable and/or stress.

**Establish routines** Help students set consistent routines, providing a stable framework that can aid memory.

**Facilitate physical organisation** Assist students in organising their personal space or provide storage solutions to minimise misplacement. Offer designated storage areas in classrooms or lockers to help students remember their items.

**Implement classroom reminders** End-of-day reminders about the next day's requirements can act as a helpful cue.

**Encourage creative solutions** Promote the use of personal reminders, whether through mobile alerts or tangible cues like coloured paper clips.

**Promote peer support** A buddy system where students help remind each other can be both supportive and a learning tool.

**Prioritise understanding** Choose support over penalties, aiming to uncover and address the reasons behind consistent forgetfulness.

### Teaching tip

Consistently forgetting kit and equipment can be indicative of deeper challenges a student faces. As educators, our role isn't to penalise but to understand, support and equip our students with strategies to overcome these challenges. Remember that we are looking for better, not perfect, so notice and acknowledge when things go to plan, and be understanding and supportive when they don't.

### Taking it further

Run short 'Organisation Workshops' at the start of term, introducing students to various tools and techniques that aid memory and organisation, catering specifically to those who face challenges in these areas.

# IDEA 90

# Effective homework planner use

*At first, I thought planners were just extra work. But with my ADHD it's a lifeline, helping me keep track and feel in control. Jamie, 15*

**For many students, especially those with ADHD, the secondary school landscape can seem like an overwhelming storm of assignments and deadlines. By guiding them in the strategic use of a homework planner, teachers can offer a beacon, helping them navigate these challenges with structure and confidence. They might not like it, but they need it.**

Here are some strategies you can try:

**Encourage comprehensive entries** Prompt students to jot down details like specific topics or chapters. This can provide clarity, especially important for ADHD students who might struggle with recall.

**Champion visual techniques** Suggest the use of colour coding or symbols to make the planner more intuitive. Such techniques can be particularly effective for visual learners.

**Allocate time for planner reviews** Dedicate a few minutes once a week for students to review their planners. This regular check-in can help ADHD students reinforce their organisational habits.

**Interactive planner workshops** Host sessions focused on planner strategies, integrating ADHD-friendly techniques and allowing students to share what works for them.

**Promote consistency** Emphasise that the planner's effectiveness grows with daily use, which can be crucial in establishing a predictable routine. Their planners should ideally be out in every lesson. Being able to switch between online and paper planners can be helpful, even if this means a duplication.

### Teaching tip

Be patient and flexible. ADHD students might take a bit longer to adapt to using a planner consistently. Celebrate small victories and offer encouragement. Each step forward is a testament to their resilience and your support.

# IDEA 91

# Forgotten homework

Behind every forgotten homework assignment is a myriad of challenges that our ADHD students face daily. *Mr. Henderson, Year 10 Maths Teacher*

**Completing homework may seem like a basic expectation, but for students with ADHD it's often a maze of executive, sensory and digital challenges. Delving into the reasons behind this can empower educators to provide targeted, effective support.**

Here are some strategies you can try:

**Recognise executive functioning challenges** ADHD-related difficulties in planning and organisation can make homework tasks challenging.

**Acknowledge sensory struggles** ADHD students often grapple with multiple stimuli; creating a classroom environment that minimises distractions can help them focus on assignments.

**Manage digital distractions** While tools like 'Show my Homework' are useful, be aware of the potential distractions they can introduce.

**Balance tool reliance** Encourage students to use planners and digital tools, but also instil the importance of active recall and not solely depending on these aids.

**Implement visual cues** Use clear visual reminders in the classroom to keep homework tasks at the forefront of students' minds.

**Engage in active confirmation** After noting down assignments, have students verbally confirm or discuss them to reinforce memory.

**Optimise digital platforms** Integrate engaging reminders or related quizzes into online homework platforms to enhance focus.

**Establish routine check-ins** Consistently review homework tasks at the start or end of lessons to embed them in students' memory.

### Taking it further

Organise short 'Homework Strategy' sessions where students can share their best practices and learn new techniques to manage and remember their assignments effectively.

# IDEA 92

# Homework challenges

Doing homework at home feels like climbing a mountain. Everything seems harder, longer and more confusing. *Oliver, 16*

**Completing homework is a universal student expectation, but for those with ADHD it can represent a labyrinth of challenges, ranging from time management to the absence of immediate feedback. To effectively support these students, educators must decode the underlying issues and implement tailored strategies.**

Here are some strategies you can try:

**Acknowledge extended effort** ADHD students often require more time for the same task at home compared to in the classroom.

**Embrace task segmentation** Split assignments into smaller, manageable portions to provide a clearer roadmap for students.

**Provide visual aids** Offer structured templates to assist in task initiation and progression.

**Understand the loss of structure** The shift from a structured classroom to the self-directed environment at home can be daunting. Acknowledge potential distractions at home and discuss strategies with students to minimise these. Strategies include healthy snacking, an instrumental playlist, studying with a friend online or in person.

**Bridge the feedback gap** Implement periodic check-ins or platforms where students can seek clarifications outside of classroom hours.

**Promote structured study spaces** Where possible, encourage using dedicated study areas at home that are free from major distractions.

**Introduce time management tools** Offer tools or apps that assist in time allocation and adherence.

**Advocate for homework clubs** Offer optional school-based study sessions, ensuring they are supportive environments and not punitive measures.

> **Taking it further**
>
> Organise a parent–teacher session focused on understanding ADHD homework challenges, fostering a collaborative approach between educators and parents to support students effectively. See Fintan O'Regan's 'Homework: Heaven or Hell?' article for more information to guide the session: www.fintanoregan.com/homework-heaven-or-hell/.

**IDEA 93**

# Handing in homework on time

Completing the assignment is half the battle; remembering to hand it in is the final, crucial step. Yet, for many of our ADHD students, this step can be unexpectedly challenging. *Mrs. Patel, English Department Head*

**For many students, particularly those with ADHD, the journey of homework doesn't end with completion. The seemingly simple act of handing it in can become an unexpected hurdle, often compounded by feelings of shame when it's submitted late.**

Here are some strategies you can try:

**Consistent submission points** Establish a routine for homework collection, whether it's a specific tray at the start of class or a dedicated point in the lesson.

**Extensions** Giving extended deadlines can be helpful, but be mindful that if things slip too far, the journey back can be impossible. However, done and in is better than not in, so you will have to take a view on this.

**Visual reminders** Use visual cues like a board or chart, listing homework due for that day or week, providing a tangible reminder at the start or end of class.

**Digital prompts** If using online platforms, set automated reminders for due dates, giving students an additional nudge. They can also set their own reminders on their phones, which develops a life skill that can prove invaluable.

**Buddy system** Pair students up to remind and check in with each other regarding homework submissions. This shared responsibility can enhance accountability.

**Empathetic approach** Foster a classroom environment where they can communicate their challenges without fear of undue reprimand.

### Teaching tip

Remember, the goal is to encourage consistent submission without amplifying feelings of shame or inadequacy. Celebrate the effort and completion, while offering supportive strategies for timely submission. The balance of acknowledgement and guidance can be a game-changer for our ADHD students.

# IDEA 94

# School attendance difficulties

Attendance challenges are multifaceted, especially for our ADHD students. It's essential we move beyond labels and truly understand the 'push' and 'pull' factors influencing their school experience.
*Ms. Lawson, Head of Pastoral Care*

**Attendance difficulties in ADHD students are often misunderstood, with many quick to label them as 'school avoidant'. However, a closer look reveals a combination of factors pushing them away from school and pulling them towards the comfort of home, and understanding this dynamic is crucial.**

### Teaching tip

Every student's attendance challenge is unique, and as educators, we must be willing to understand the root causes without judgement. By addressing both the 'push' and 'pull' factors and fostering a supportive environment, we can bridge the attendance gap and help our ADHD students thrive academically and emotionally. See the Bloomsbury Education website for more guidance on school attendance difficulties.

Here are some strategies you can try:

**Beyond assumptions** Abandon preconceived notions of 'school avoidance' and approach each student's attendance challenges with an open mind and genuine curiosity.

**Identifying 'push' factors** Understand the elements within the school environment that might make attendance challenging, such as sensory overloads, academic pressures or peer dynamics.

**Recognising 'pull' factors** Acknowledge the comforts and securities of home that might draw a student away from school, be it a safe space, emotional support, or avoidance of school-related stressors.

**Open dialogue** Foster a trusting relationship where students can openly discuss their feelings and concerns about school, ensuring they feel validated and understood.

**Collaborative solutions** Engage with parents, caregivers and other professionals to develop strategies that address both 'push' and 'pull' factors, creating a more welcoming and supportive school environment.

# Working with parents and professionals

**Part 10**

## IDEA 95

# School exclusions

Exclusions often start with small events and minor disruptions, which can quickly snowball, especially for our ADHD students. We must be proactive, understanding, and find ways to address root causes before they escalate. *Mr. Roberts, Deputy Headteacher*

**ADHD students are at a higher risk of school exclusions, both fixed-term and permanent. Often these exclusions don't result from major incidents but rather accumulate from repeated low-level disruptions that aren't effectively addressed.**

Here are some strategies you can try:

**Recognise early signs** Stay alert to recurring patterns of low-level disruption in ADHD students, understanding that these can be precursors to more significant issues if they are not addressed.

**Understand ADHD dynamics** Recognise that the impulsive and inattentive behaviours characteristic of ADHD can inadvertently lead to disruptions, even if they aren't intentional.

**Open communication** Foster a dialogue with the student to understand the root causes of their behaviour, ensuring they feel heard and supported in finding solutions.

**Interventions over punishments** Prioritise supportive interventions, like behaviour support plans or tailored strategies, over punitive measures that can exacerbate exclusion.

**Collaborative approach** Engage parents, caregivers and specialists in creating a supportive ecosystem for the student, addressing behavioural concerns while reinforcing positive behaviours.

> **Teaching tip**
>
> Exclusions can have long-term repercussions on a student's academic and emotional wellbeing. By understanding the unique challenges faced by ADHD students and prioritising supportive interventions over punitive measures, we can help prevent exclusions and ensure every student has a fair chance at success.

**IDEA 96**

# Zero tolerance behaviour policies

*I know the rules are there for a reason, but sometimes it feels like they're stacked against me because of my ADHD. Zoe, 13*

**Zero tolerance behaviour policies aim to create a consistent and orderly environment in schools. However, for students with ADHD, these strict policies can often pose unique challenges, making it essential for educators to find a balanced approach.**

Here are some strategies you can try:

**Acknowledge the challenge** There are many reasons why ADHD students might unintentionally breach zero tolerance policies, including impulsivity, inattentiveness, hyperactivity, difficulty remembering, and many more.

**Clarify expectations** Regularly and clearly remind all students about the school behaviour policies, ensuring they're fully aware of expectations.

**Proactive interventions** Implement early interventions and support systems tailored for ADHD students, reducing the likelihood of policy breaches.

**Setting them up to succeed** Consider where students are likely to breach a rule, and discuss strategies with them that give them the best likelihood of adhering to the requirements.

**Open dialogue** Maintain communication with ADHD students, understanding their perspective and challenges, and collaboratively brainstorming strategies to help them navigate the school's policies.

**Flexibility within framework** While upholding the school's policies, seek opportunities for **reasonable adjustments** that can cater to the unique needs of ADHD students without compromising overall school discipline.

> **Teaching tip**
>
> Zero tolerance doesn't mean zero understanding. As educators, we can uphold our school's behaviour policies while ensuring that ADHD students are supported, understood and included in positive ways. Acknowledge that it is hard, and doesn't always feel fair. Yes, ADHD might be the reason a student is struggling, but what are we going to do about it, together?

# IDEA 97

# Reasonable adjustments

Making **reasonable adjustments** for our ADHD students is not about giving them an easy way out. It's about levelling the playing field so they can reach their full potential. *Ms. Thompson, Inclusion Lead*

**Reasonable adjustments are essential modifications or accommodations made to support students with ADHD in their learning journey. While these adjustments aim to address specific challenges, it's crucial to implement them in a way that supports without further isolating or marginalising the student.**

Here are some strategies you can try:

**Identify specific needs** Collaborate with SENCOs, parents and the student to identify the unique challenges and areas where adjustments are required.

**Tailored adjustments** Implement individualised modifications, such as extended time for assignments, preferential seating, or the use of assistive technology, based on the student's needs.

**Promote inclusion** Ensure that adjustments don't isolate the student. For instance, if a student uses assistive technology, introduce it to the whole class as a potential tool for everyone, highlighting its benefits.

**Ongoing feedback** Regularly check in with the ADHD student to gather feedback on the effectiveness of the adjustments and make necessary changes.

**Educate and advocate** Foster an inclusive classroom environment by educating all students about ADHD and wider neurodiversity. Explain the reason for specific adjustments, promoting understanding and reducing potential stigmatisation.

### Taking it further

As educators, it's essential to view the challenges of **low-level persistent disruption (LLPD)** through the broader context of children's rights. The Equality Act 2010 mandates that we must not discriminate against, harass, or victimise students with disabilities, including conditions like ADHD. By penalising these students for manifestations of their neurodiversity, we risk infringing upon their legal rights to fair treatment. Addressing LLPD without considering its roots in neurodiversity not only compromises our commitment to inclusive education but also challenges our legal and ethical responsibilities to uphold these crucial rights. You may not be able to do anything about school policies right now, but as educators and leaders of the future, I hope this is useful to know.

**IDEA 98**

# Balanced and constructive school reports

When I read my report, I want to see how I've grown and where I can improve, not just be reminded of my struggles. *Layla, 16*

**A school report is a crucial communication tool between educators and parents. For students with ADHD, these reports should be both enlightening and encouraging, focusing on progress, strengths and constructive feedback rather than just reiterating known ADHD-related challenges.**

Here are some strategies you can try:

**Highlight strengths** Start with the positives. Mention specific areas where the student has excelled or shown improvement.

**Be specific** Instead of generic comments like 'needs to concentrate', provide specific examples, such as 'has shown increased focus during group discussions'.

**Offer constructive feedback** Replace comments like 'remember equipment' with actionable advice such as 'using a daily checklist might help with equipment organisation'.

**Acknowledge effort** Recognise the student's efforts, even if the outcomes aren't always perfect. Mention instances where they've tried hard or shown resilience.

**Avoid redundancies** Steer clear of repeatedly mentioning known ADHD-related challenges. Once acknowledged, focus on other areas.

**Collaborate with SENCOs** Engage with SENCOs to ensure that the feedback is tailored and sensitive.

**Include extracurricular achievements** Highlight the student's achievements outside the classroom, recognising their holistic development.

### Teaching tip

A balanced report not only informs but also motivates and empowers. By focusing on the complete picture – strengths, challenges and potential – we can craft reports for our ADHD students that are both enlightening and encouraging. This is your chance to say something that shows you know and value this student. Take that opportunity – you may be the only teacher that does!

# IDEA 99

# Constructive parents' evenings

*I want to leave a parents' evening feeling informed, understood and confident that we're all working towards the same goal for my child.*
*Mr. Ahmed, Parent of Year 9 Student*

**Parents' evenings offer a pivotal moment for educators and parents to connect, share insights and chart a path forward for the student. For ADHD students, these meetings can be even more significant, providing a chance to build a united front that acknowledges challenges while focusing on strengths and solutions.**

Here are some strategies you can try:

**Begin positively** Start the conversation by acknowledging the student's hard work, resilience and determination, even if results aren't always ideal.

**Be solution-focused** Instead of listing challenges, discuss potential strategies and solutions. For example, rather than saying 'struggles with attention', you might suggest 'visual aids have been helpful in maintaining focus'.

**Open dialogue** Encourage parents to share their insights, experiences and strategies that work at home.

**Avoid assumptions** Recognise that every ADHD experience is unique. Avoid making blanket statements or assumptions and listen to the parent's perspective.

**Set realistic expectations** Be clear about short-term and longer-term goals to align expectations.

**Build a relationship** Use the meeting as an opportunity to establish trust and rapport with the parent. Express genuine care and commitment to the student's wellbeing and success.

**End on a positive note** Conclude the meeting by reiterating the student's strengths and the collaborative plan moving forward.

### Teaching tip

Parents' evenings are a bridge between home and school. By fostering a positive, open and collaborative relationship with parents, we can ensure that our ADHD students receive consistent and constructive support in both environments.

### Taking it further

Offer parents resources, such as reading materials, workshops or support groups, that can help them better understand and support their child's ADHD journey.

**IDEA 100**

# ADHD assessment reporting scales for teachers

*I may seem okay on the outside, but it's a constant battle to stay focused and engaged. My teachers' honest feedback on those forms can make all the difference in getting the right support. Aiden, 13*

**When completing ADHD assessment scales, teachers have the responsibility to bring to light the hidden struggles of students. Even if a student has developed coping mechanisms, the underlying challenges should be transparently communicated to provide a clear picture for professionals.**

Here are some strategies you can try:
**Highlight underlying struggles** Recognise and report the efforts students put into coping strategies, like using fidgets. Their strategies shouldn't mask the actual challenge.
**Stay objective yet empathetic** Be factual, but also consider the student's inner battles and how they might be masking their ADHD symptoms.
**Use the scale thoughtfully** Typically, diagnosticians will ask you to complete a 1–5 rating scale based on the DSM criteria, which should be used to accurately reflect the student's daily experiences. For more information on diagnosing ADHD, see the Bloomsbury Education website.
**Make explanations count** Ensure that every word paints a clear picture of the student's struggles.
**Avoid sugar coating** This isn't the time for diplomacy. If there's a challenge, state it clearly.
**Collaborate with peers** Talk to colleagues who interact with the student. They might offer insights you haven't noticed.
**Refrain from comparisons** Focus solely on the student in question.
**Seek guidance if needed** If a particular question is challenging or unclear, consult with the assessing clinician for clarity.

### Teaching tip

Our feedback on ADHD assessment scales can significantly impact the interventions and support a student receives. It's our duty to ensure our feedback is honest and reflective of the student's true experiences.

# Glossary

**ABCD method**: A behavioural strategy for understanding and influencing student behaviour. It stands for Antecedent (the context for the behaviour), Behaviour (the behaviour itself), Consequence (the result of the behaviour), and Documentation (recording the observations to inform future interventions).

**Adverse childhood experiences (ACEs)**: Traumatic events that occur during childhood and can have lasting effects on an individual's mental and physical health. Recognising and addressing ACEs can be crucial for the supportive development of students with ADHD.

**Auditory processing disorder**: A condition where the brain does not properly process sounds, especially speech. Students with this disorder may require alternative teaching methods to support their learning.

**Attribution (healthy and unhealthy)**: The process of explaining the causes of behaviours and events. Healthy attribution involves recognising and attributing successes or failures to appropriate causes, fostering resilience and a growth mindset. Unhealthy attribution refers to the tendency to misattribute successes or failures, potentially harming self-esteem and motivation. Educators should guide students with ADHD towards healthy attribution.

**Confirmation bias**: The tendency to interpret new evidence as confirmation of one's existing beliefs or theories. In an educational setting, this bias can affect how teachers and peers perceive the actions and responses of students with ADHD.

**Delayed gratification**: The ability to resist the temptation for an immediate reward and wait for a later one. Developing this skill can help students with ADHD increase self-control and improve long-term outcomes.

**Eisenhower box**: Also known as the urgent–important matrix, this tool helps prioritise tasks based on their urgency and importance, a useful skill for students with ADHD to manage their responsibilities.

**Encoding**: The process of transforming information into a memory. Techniques to enhance encoding can benefit students with ADHD by improving their ability to retain and recall information.

**Executive function**: Cognitive processes including working memory, flexible thinking and self-control. Students with ADHD may struggle with these and can benefit from strategies to enhance their executive functioning.

**Gantt chart**: A visual planning tool that outlines project timelines and tasks. Gantt charts can aid students with ADHD in breaking down assignments into manageable steps.

**Healthy attribution:** See attribution.

**Interoception**: The sense of the internal state of the body, such as hunger and thirst. Students with ADHD might need support in recognising and interpreting these internal cues.

**Low-level persistent disruption (LLPD)**: Continuous minor disruptive behaviours in the classroom setting. Identifying and addressing these disruptions is important for maintaining a conducive learning environment for all students, including those with ADHD.

**Neural pathways**: The links between neurons in the brain that enable communication and the formation of memories. Understanding these can be key in developing educational strategies for students with ADHD.

**Neurotypical**: A term used to describe individuals whose brain development and activity are within the society's norm. Understanding this helps in contrasting and accommodating the needs of neurodiverse students, including those with ADHD.

**Oppositional defiant disorder (ODD)**: A behaviour disorder characterised by anger, irritability and defiance.

**Proprioception**: The sensory ability to perceive body movement and position. For students with ADHD, enhancing proprioceptive feedback can aid in self-regulation and coordination.

**Reasonable adjustments**: Modifications or accommodations provided in educational settings to support students with disabilities, such as ADHD, ensuring they have equal access to education and can fully participate.

**Restorative practice/justice**: An approach that focuses on the rehabilitation of offenders through reconciliation with victims and the community at large. When applied in schools, it can help students with ADHD learn from their actions and repair relationships.

**SMART**: An acronym for goal-setting that stands for Specific, Measurable, Achievable, Relevant and Time-bound. SMART goals can help students with ADHD to focus and achieve their objectives.

**The great dopamine chase**: Author's own term, referring to the pursuit of activities that release dopamine, a neurotransmitter associated with pleasure and reward, which may be sought out more by individuals with ADHD.

**Uber empathy**: The author's own term, describing a heightened sense of empathy, which could affect how students with ADHD interact socially and emotionally.

**Urgent–important matrix**: Also known as the Eisenhower box, a tool for prioritising tasks based on their urgency and importance, which can be particularly beneficial for students with ADHD in managing their time and tasks.

**Unhealthy attribution:** See attribution.

**Zone of proximal development (ZPD)**: ZPD is a foundational concept by psychologist Lev Vygotsky, which identifies the range between what a learner can do independently and what they can do with assistance. Optimal learning occurs within this range. For educators, the ZPD underscores the importance of tailored instruction and the value of scaffolding. Teaching within a student's ZPD can enhance their learning experience, ensuring that they are consistently challenged and supported.